SUCCESS
Affirmations

SUCCESS
Affirmations

52 Weeks for Living a Passionate and Purposeful *Life*

Jack Canfield
with Ram Ganglani and Kelly Johnson

Health Communications, Inc.
Deerfield Beach, Florida

www.hcibooks.com

Library of Congress Cataloging-in-Publication Data
is available through the Library of Congress

© 2017 Jack Canfield

ISBN-13: 978-07573-2012-5 (Paperback)
ISBN-10: 07573-2012-0 (Paperback)
ISBN-13: 978-07573-2025-5 (ePub)
ISBN-10: 07573-2025-2 (ePub)

Publisher: Health Communications, Inc.
        3201 S.W. 15th Street
        Deerfield Beach, FL 33442–8190

Cover design by Larissa Hise Henoch
Interior design and formatting by Lawna Patterson Oldfield

CONTENTS

INTRODUCTION

*B*e careful what you wish for. You've probably heard that phrase often. But did you know there's actual science behind that advice? Researchers in the field of neuroscience now know that the brain is a goal-seeking organism. Whatever idea, image, or outcome you think about, talk about, and feel strongly about, *you will bring about*. Of course, far from being a dark and gloomy prospect, this powerful scientific phenomenon actually has the ability to improve every area of your life—in ways you can't even imagine today.

There's even a tool you can use to focus your thoughts and accelerate the process of achieving your goals. It's called an *affirmation*: a statement that describes a goal *as if it's already been achieved*.

What does an affirmation look like?

I'm blissfully watching the sunset from the veranda of my estate in Tuscany is one example. *I'm joyfully depositing a $100,000 royalty check from my bestselling book* is another. They're statements

1

that stretch your mind with new thoughts and lavish images—and actually work with the brain's own processes to bring about change in your life. When you bombard your brain with colorful pictures, exciting details, and joyful emotions of what will be, a phenomenon called *cognitive dissonance* occurs in your mind. Cognitive dissonance is the mental discomfort—the uncomfortable feelings—you get when you hold two conflicting beliefs or ideas: (1) your life as you're living it today and (2) your life as you would like it to be in the future. When you continue the limiting behaviors that got you to where you are today or believe strongly that somehow you're not capable of getting what you want—*then you suddenly begin using daily affirmations to visualize a better life*—you create a form of mental tension that your brain will do everything in its power to resolve *by actually creating the better, more desirable lifestyle for you!*

Psychologist Leon Festinger, author of *A Theory of Cognitive Dissonance,* compares this process to how your brain reacts when you're hungry: It sends signals to your body to eat. In other words, it causes you to take necessary steps to resolve your hunger. In the same way, when you begin using affirmations to visualize your exciting new future with compelling pictures and emotions, your brain will likewise cause you to take those steps necessary to bring about that exciting new future.

Bombarding your brain with thoughts of a better life through daily visualization and verbalization will actually force your brain to resolve the cognitive dissonance it dislikes. Affirmations are those highly visual and emotionally compelling statements you can use daily to visualize a better life.

Everything great that has ever happened to humanity . . . has begun as a single thought in someone's mind.

—YIANNIS CHRYSSOMALLIS
Known professionally as Yanni, the composer,
pianist, and music producer

How affirmations can change your life

Since you're reading this book, you've probably decided you want your life to be different in some way. Whether it's a more exciting career, better finances, loving and supportive relationships, world travel, more vibrant health, or just the luxury of a calm and organized life that works for you, there are steps you can take toward getting there.

This book is about those steps.

Not only does it include recommended affirmations to get you started on this powerful daily habit, it introduces you to a set of 52 powerful principles that the world's top achievers have used for decades to excel in business, the arts, sports, philanthropy, politics, and more. These are principles that I have studied, taught, and applied to my own life for nearly 40 years—and that Ram Ganglani has used for three decades to achieve success in business, philanthropy, and private life. We've also seen these principles work in hundreds of thousands of lives besides our own. Using the framework of these proven principles, *Success*

Affirmations is therefore not just a book of good ideas and positive thoughts, it's also a book of proven steps for creating success and happiness.

These principles always work, if you always work the principles

In fact, if you mastered just *one* principle a week, as this book will guide you to do, you could literally transform your life in just one year.

But the key is that *you* must take responsibility for implementing these principles in your life. Creating a daily habit of reciting and internalizing your affirmations is just one of these principles—which you'll find on page 45 entitled "Week 10: Use Affirmations to Release the Brakes." But make no mistake: you alone have to do the work of implementing these principles in your life—you can't delegate them or skip over the ones you don't like. In fact, each one is integral to achieving overall success. It's just like writing a book. Before you can even start the process, you have to learn to read and write, you have to learn structure and syntax, you have to learn to put words into a sentence and sentences into paragraphs and paragraphs into chapters. If you leave a step out, the book will make no sense and readers will not benefit from it. Imagine a book with no periods or commas, no paragraphs or chapters! It just doesn't work.

In the same way, each principle and its accompanying affirmations are key components to creating a successful and happy life. *Your* life. No one else can create your goals, build your dreams, and determine your future. Motivational philosopher Jim Rohn put it this way, "You can't hire someone else to do your push-ups for you."

Whether you're exercising, setting goals, meditating, studying, or even sleeping, some things you just have to do for yourself to get any benefit from them. And like the principles I teach in this book and the affirmations you will use to instill those principles and their benefits in your consciousness, if you'll simply make a commitment to applying them week after week and stick with it, you'll reap extraordinary rewards.

40 years of living these principles and affirmations prove that they work

Albert Einstein once said, "The world as we have created it is a process of our thinking. It cannot be changed without changing our thinking." Affirmations are the tool that, day by day, will slowly change your thinking. Make even greater effort by implementing these principles in your life, and things will begin to happen that you never thought possible.

It happened for me—and this is Jack talking.

Growing up in Wheeling, West Virginia, I lived in an average home. My dad was a workaholic and my mom, an alcoholic. I earned cash during summers working in my grandfather's florist business and as a lifeguard at the local pool. I made it through Harvard University on a partial scholarship—serving breakfast at the campus dining commons to pay for books, clothes, and dates. During my last year of graduate school, I got a part-time teaching job that paid $120 every two weeks. That had to cover my rent and other expenses. To say that I was often broke would be an understatement. When money was tight, I survived on what I called my "21¢ dinners"—a can of tomato paste, garlic salt, water, and a box of spaghetti noodles.

I was living on a very low rung of the economic ladder. How I made it to graduation is anybody's guess.

But some time later, after I had started my career as a high school teacher on the south side of Chicago, I was offered a job at a unique foundation where I would be teaching others the principles espoused by its self-made millionaire founder, W. Clement Stone. I reveled in the opportunity to not only learn these principles for myself but also help others change their lives. That was the beginning of 40 years of learning, testing, and teaching the principles I'll reveal to you in this book. I went on to implement them in my own life—eventually becoming a multimillionaire, authoring countless bestselling books, originating the *Chicken Soup for the Soul®* book series, building several successful companies, and becoming a top success coach and transformational trainer.

Every principle for success in this book is one that I personally learned through experience and developed as part of the curriculum I now teach in more than 100 countries. Through the years, I have never stopped learning, growing, creating new goals, and achieving them. And that's what I want for you, too. The truth is, anyone can consistently produce never-before-seen results in their life, as long as they're willing to put the principles to work.

Decide what you want, believe in yourself, and use the affirmations we'll give you to begin living the principles and habits you'll learn in this book.

How to get the most out of this book

In addition to helping you focus on achieving your goals, it's also been proven that positive thoughts reinforce and increase the good energy vibrations you send out into the Universe—attracting beneficial energy back to you. It's a law of the Universe that success, abundance, joy, mindfulness, and wealth increase exponentially when we set ourselves on a course of positivity.

Affirmations are a big part of that.

They also help to rewire our thought patterns and emotional responses—creating new pathways in the brain that, over time, replace old patterns that keep us stagnant and unproductive. Using positive affirmations isn't just a tool for flooding your mind with positive self-talk, it's also a tool that will help you conquer your fears, overcome obstacles, and circumvent roadblocks that keep you from achieving your dreams.

In each chapter of this book, you'll discover three positive affirmations you can use to empower yourself—together with the success principle behind them so you can put them into practice. We recommend that you choose one of these affirmations that speaks to a goal or need you're experiencing right now, and make that your daily meditation. Spend ten minutes every morning saying it aloud and visualizing it as if it were already completed. See yourself in your mind's eye—living as if you've already met that goal. Summon the emotions you'd be feeling— the joyfulness, excitement, sense of security or confidence. Add other sensory and sound experiences to your meditation that mimic what you'd be experiencing when your goals are met— whether it's the wind on your face or the sound of applause or the thrust of a private jet as it initiates lift-off. Feel the emotion.

If you like, you can grab some index cards and colored felt markers to illustrate the affirmations on pocket-sized flash cards. But you should also begin writing down *new* affirmations that fit your specific goals and life circumstances, following the guidelines on page 48. At the end of each day, spend ten minutes on the same affirmations before you go to bed, and your subconscious mind will continue to focus on these goals throughout the night. Move on to other affirmations we've provided in each chapter as you focus on putting that principle into action.

Week by week, your life will begin to change.

Just as we've seen in countless people who've learned these principles, you have an entire life of abundance and joy waiting for you. Start using affirmations and claim it!

Week
1

Take 100% Responsibility for Your Future

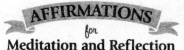

AFFIRMATIONS
for
Meditation and Reflection

I am easily improving my life—moving with ease from where I am now to where I want to be.

I am confidently creating better circumstances and expanding opportunity for myself—responding with intelligence to events as they occur.

I am choosing to change my thoughts, images, and behaviors to respond differently and produce better outcomes.

We don't naturally want to take responsibility for our lives.
We want to give the responsibility to someone else.
We blame them when our lives aren't good.

—DONALD MILLER
Author of *A Million Miles in a Thousand Years:*
How I Learned to Live a Better Story

*L*et's start with some really good news: You have total control over the thoughts you think, the images you visualize, and the actions you take. How you use these three things determines everything you experience in life. On your journey to a life of abundance, fulfillment, and success, taking 100% responsibility for your future is the starting line.

Here is where you are today, and *there* is where you want to be—it is the fulfillment of your hopes and dreams. It is the realization of your life purpose and your ultimate goals, and I am going to show you the way to get there. Together, we are going to embark on an exciting journey that is based upon using daily affirmations—positive statements that affirm who you are, what you believe, and the fact that you already have everything you need at your disposal to succeed in reaching your goals. You may not think that you do, but I am going to show you how to change your thinking and build a blueprint for success.

I am easily improving my life—
moving with ease from where I am
now to where I want to be.

*P*ositive energy will get your day off to a great start. Set a few minutes aside every morning and repeat your affirmation aloud with conviction and intention. Do this again at night and let your subconscious mind apply that positive energy as you sleep. When you let it empower your thoughts and dreams during the night, you are training it to think differently—to automatically lean toward positive opportunity and action while you are awake.

Repeating affirmations will help you consciously improve as long as you take full responsibility for your life—that means every success, every failure, and every indecisive thought or action you have experienced. Regardless of the circumstance, placing the blame on the event or outcome won't make a difference because it's your response to it that is the game-changer—and your response, whether it's your thoughts, images, or behaviors, is totally up to you. The truth is, you don't have to settle for anything in life because you can keep changing your response to the circumstance you may face until you get the result you want. If you don't like your current results, simply begin to do something different.

I am confidently creating better circumstances and expanding opportunity for myself— responding with intelligence to events as they occur.

*I*t's easy sometimes to think things "just happen" to you— that you were an innocent bystander or an unwitting participant. Don't let yourself be tricked into playing that game. You are the one creating or allowing it to happen. Start paying attention to what I call "yellow alerts." There are always signals that tell you something is off or something is about to happen. If you don't pay attention to the internal and external yellow alerts, you will needlessly suffer. External yellow alerts are things like news trends that your industry is fading or the smell of alcohol on your teenager's breath. Internal alerts are things like gut feelings, intuitive messages, and feelings of stress, tension, or pain. Paying closer attention to your internal and external yellow alerts will enable you to change your actions or responses once you become aware of them.

Let this thought encourage you: Life becomes much easier when you take control of your own destiny. Don't accept that things "just happen" to you—choose to create the life you really want!

> *I am choosing to change my thoughts, images, and behaviors to respond differently and produce better outcomes.*

Week 2

Be Clear Why You're Here

AFFIRMATIONS
for
Meditation and Reflection

I am joyful and fulfilled, living in perfect alignment with my life purpose.

I am visualizing a perfect world where everyone is living in harmony and experiencing their life purpose to the fullest.

I am passionately and joyfully pursuing the unique calling in my life—every day moving closer and closer to achieving my goals.

13

> *Decide upon your major definite purpose in life and then organize all your activities around it.*
>
> —BRIAN TRACY
> Author of *Change Your Thinking, Change Your Life*

*E*veryone has a unique calling in their life—something only you can do, something only you have the unique skills and wisdom to accomplish. Identifying, acknowledging, and honoring this life purpose may be the most important thing that you do on your way to creating a successful life. It's certainly one of the most fulfilling. But, without a clear understanding of what you're here on this Earth to do, and pursuing that purpose with passion and enthusiasm, you will almost certainly fall short of any goal you set.

Most people haven't a clue why they are on this Earth. Maybe they think knowing isn't really important, or they are waiting for a personal awakening, or they're hoping that the answer mysteriously appears on their daily to-do list. The problem with *not knowing* isn't just that you lose time making U-turns, getting stuck, and backtracking to the fork in the road—but that you get lost, sidetracked, or become stagnant. When you lose your sense of direction, it can cause untold emotional setbacks and turmoil, leaving you feeling hopeless, useless, or frustrated.

> *I am joyful and fulfilled, living in perfect alignment with my life purpose.*

*I*n my many workshops and books, I offer exercises to help people identify their life purpose and assure they find meaning and direction.

THE LIFE PURPOSE EXERCISE

1) List two of your unique personal qualities, such as *leadership* and *innovation*.

2) List one or two ways you enjoy expressing those qualities when interacting with others, such as *to support* and *to inspire*.

3) Assume the world is perfect and that each of us is living our unique calling. What does the world look and feel like?
Example: Everyone is working in their ideal field, in harmony with each other and without conflict or damage to the Earth.

4) Combine your answers above into a single statement that defines *your life purpose* and tells how it contributes to an ideal world.
Example: To use my leadership qualities to inspire and support innovative entrepreneurs who are building sustainable businesses.

I am visualizing a perfect world where everyone is living in harmony and experiencing their life purpose to the fullest.

These short exercises should help you discover that your inner guidance system is fueled by your greatest joys when they are in alignment with your purpose. But let's take it one step further: Write down the common elements of your most joyful experiences from the first exercise so you remember them. Next, write your life purpose statement from the second exercise and hang it where you will see it every day. Read your statement aloud every morning and at bedtime—the words should make you feel inspired.

When you are doing what you love to do, you are also accomplishing what you're good at and what is important to you. Your life will become more balanced and open to opportunities, people, and resources that will benefit you. As you begin living your life purpose, there's a synergy and universal magnetism that begins working within you and toward you. The things you do will automatically serve others and people will feel your positive energy.

Make a commitment to determine your life purpose at all costs—you simply can't achieve abundance and success without knowing why you are here on this Earth.

> *I am passionately and joyfully pursuing the unique calling in my life—every day moving closer and closer to achieving my goals.*

Week 3

Decide What You Want to Be, Do, and Have

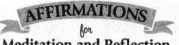

for
Meditation and Reflection

I am defining in compelling detail what I want to be, what I want to do, and what I want to have.

I am letting go of childhood programming that holds me back and replacing it with positive thoughts and images about my compelling future.

I am focused on what I truly want for my life based on my own values and life experience.

17

> *The indispensable first step to getting the*
> *things you want out of life is this:*
> *Decide what you want.*

—BEN STEIN
Actor and author

If you were to describe "success," what would it look like? No doubt it would include all the things you want to experience, accomplish, and acquire—including those things on your "bucket list." Unfortunately, many people have the whole scenario backward—they start with what they want to have first, then, later on in life, they find themselves at a point where they realize they don't know either why they are here or what their life purpose is. They don't have the inner success they expected—and the deep sense of joy that should come from living their life purpose is completely missing.

Let this thought encourage you: No matter what your age or circumstance, you can always decide to do things differently. You can start the process of deciding what you want.

I am defining in clear and compelling detail
what I want to be, what I want to do,
and what I want to have.

D o you know that you were born with the seed of who you were meant to become already inside you? You were also born without inhibitions or fears—you cried when you were hungry, you crawled all over the place, you laughed at silly noises and faces. As you got older, you were told to stop crying, to grow up, to stop being selfish. You learned to ignore the things you really wanted and to fit in with what your parents, teachers, or society told you was best. Now it's time to un-learn and replace these childhood decisions.

Michelangelo, the renaissance sculptor and painter who spent four years lying on his back painting the ceiling of the Sistine Chapel, said, "The greater danger for most of us is not that our aim is too high and we miss it, but that it is too low and we reach it." Wow!

When we allow others to dictate our "wants" or determine what we should do with our lives, we end up settling for whatever is handed to us, or worse, pursuing a life we simply don't enjoy. This can lead to depression, anxiety, stress, and a whole list of negative outcomes. Your life is exactly that—yours. No one can determine what your life experience should be—other than you.

> *I am letting go of childhood programming that holds me back and replacing it with positive thoughts and images about my compelling future.*

o help you decide what you really want, try these two exercises that I have been using in my workshops for a number of years.

1) **Make an "I want" list:**

Write down 30 things you want to do, 30 things you want to have, and 30 things you want to be before you die. The big things—cars and houses—will probably be at the top of the list, but as you work your way down, you'll rediscover your core values like *making a difference.*

2) **Make a "20 things I love to do" list:**

Think you can't make a living doing the things you love? When you write them down and really think through what it would be like to pursue those activities every day— and how others pursue them already—you'll discover you *can* make a career out of doing what you love!

Find a place with a comfortable, quiet environment, and then clarify your vision of the ideal life being clear and specific. Include these seven areas in your ideal life: work and career, finances, fun and recreation, health and fitness, personal goals, relationships, and your contribution to the larger community.

I am focused on what I truly want for my life based on my own values and life experience.

Week 4

Believe It's Possible

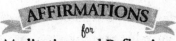

I am releasing beliefs and negative statements that limit me and creating new, positive statements that tell me my ideal future is possible.

I choose to believe things are possible, even when I don't know how they will happen.

I am working toward fulfilling my goals every day and I easily move past those times when my expectations are not met.

When anyone tells me I can't do anything . . .
I'm just not listening anymore.

—FLORENCE "FLO JO" GRIFFITH JOYNER
Considered the fastest woman of all time based on the
world records she set in track and field in 1988

ractically every psychology class in the world teaches a concept called *expectancy theory:* the idea that we respond to events in life based on what the brain expects to happen, which it's learned from our prior life experience. In other words, people usually decide to behave in a certain way based on expected results.

Where we run into trouble, though, is when we let negative prior experiences and a lack of self-confidence control our decisions; when that happens, we act a certain way and get a negative outcome. But what if, instead, you intentionally held positive expectations in your mind? You could achieve exactly what you want much more easily.

Whenever a difficult situation or negative thought enters your mind, write it down. Write down what you are thinking, why it's a problem, and what has caused it. Then, break these thoughts down into smaller parts and re-imagine them as positives. Now, put the pieces back together and create a new, positive statement that helps you believe what you want is possible.

I am releasing beliefs and negative statements
that limit me and creating new, positive statements
that tell me my ideal future is possible.

There are two roadblocks that hold us back from achieving our goals and making good decisions. The first one is fear of what we don't know: *What will it take to get me from here to there? How will I make ends meet in the meantime?* Those questions will discourage you if you let them. But all those details will fall into place if you believe in your goals and believe in yourself.

The second roadblock is what you think you know that just isn't true. Think about that. Could a lot of what you think you know actually be wrong? Relying too much on your own knowledge and experiences without questioning your assumptions is a slippery slope. You need to learn the real facts and use this information to become a *possibility thinker*.

Your mind is an amazing instrument—you can let it absorb bad or damaging information, or you can train it to produce positive thoughts (by using affirmations, for instance). You know that taking responsibility and being in control of your life is integral to achieving your goals, and you also know that you have the power to learn and un-learn thought patterns and responses at will. Only you can decide what you will accept and what you will block from your mind, so it's up to you to avoid negative and incorrect data.

> *I choose to believe things are possible, even when I don't know how they will happen.*

ℕ apoleon Hill, the author of *Think and Grow Rich* once said, "You can be anything you want to be, if only you believe with sufficient conviction and act according to your faith; for whatever the mind can conceive and believe, it can achieve."

That's truly a profound statement.

You see, it's all well and good to practice positive thinking and self-motivation, but without truly believing anything is possible, you won't get very far. Let's say you've been working toward a promotion for the last year or two, and you muster up the confidence to speak to the Vice President. You are confident in your ability and expect a positive outcome, only you don't get one, and you become discouraged. Remember that, although you believed in yourself and expected a different outcome, you are no worse off than the day before. You haven't really lost anything.

Being confident and expecting a positive outcome is not the same as instant gratification—if you're expecting an unequivocal yes for every question you ask, you're off target. What it is actually about is changing negative attitudes and thoughts and accepting the present. When you believe in yourself and believe anything is possible, opportunities will come from places and people you'd never expect, and the world will respond in astonishing ways.

> *I am working toward fulfilling my goals every day and I easily move past those times when my expectations are not met.*

Week 5

Believe in Yourself

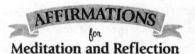

AFFIRMATIONS
for
Meditation and Reflection

I am facing each day with a positive attitude, which empowers me to truly believe that anything is possible.

I am living positively at all times and have given up using negative phrases like "I can't" because I know I can!

I am choosing every day to believe that I am worthy and deserving of success, no matter my age or my circumstances.

You weren't an accident. You weren't mass-produced.
You aren't an assembly-line product. You were deliberately
planned, specifically gifted, and lovingly positioned
on the Earth by the Master Craftsman.

—MAX LUCADO
Bestselling author

ecause you are going to be successful and create the life of your dreams, you have to *believe* you can do it—even if you can't see the whole picture of exactly how it will happen.

Developing a confident attitude and believing in yourself is a choice, regardless of the limiting beliefs and negative conditioning you may have grown up with. You must choose to believe that you can do anything you set your mind to—because you can. There are hundreds of studies and volumes of research on the human brain that show how positive self-talk, visualization, training, coaching, and practice can help retrain the brain so that we can accomplish almost anything,

If you don't develop an attitude of success and belief in yourself, you won't do what's needed. Whether you believe you can or believe you can't, your thoughts become a self-fulfilling prophecy. It's your choice to believe or not.

I am facing each day with a positive attitude,
which empowers me to truly believe
that anything is possible.

*Y*our brain is designed to solve problems and reach goals, and that means you have to give up phrases like "I can't," "I wish I were able to," and "if only I could." Those negative words disempower you and actually make you weaker.

When you were a toddler, you climbed up on anything that stood in your way. But little by little, your sense of invincibility was eroded by the negative reactions you received from your family, teachers, and friends. Eventually, you no longer believed you could conquer everything in your way.

Too often we feel the need to have others believe in us and in our dreams in order to be successful, but your decisions need to be based on your own goals and desires, not those of your parents, friends, spouse, children, and coworkers. How can you possibly follow your heart if you're sitting around worrying what other people think about you?

Dr. Daniel Amen has an 18/40/60 Rule: When you're 18, you worry about what everyone is thinking about you; when you're 40 you don't give a darn what anybody thinks of you; when you're 60, you realize that nobody is thinking about you at all. Stop wasting time worrying about what other people think and spend that time focusing on doing the things that will achieve your goals.

I am living positively at all times and have given up using negative phrases like "I can't" because I know I can!

Did you know that 20% of America's millionaires never set foot in college? Even former Vice President Dick Cheney dropped out of college! Plus, there are countless other examples of people who became successful in their field or who started a new path in life without "prerequisites" such as schooling, age, or finances—simply because they believed they could accomplish what they wanted.

Take six-year-old Ryan Hreljac for instance: Shocked to learn that children in Africa had to walk many miles every day just to fetch clean water, little Ryan raised enough money to build a well in northern Uganda by the time he was eight. Today, Ryan's Well Foundation has completed 878 water projects and 1,120 latrines in 16 countries.

- The famous chef Julia Child didn't even learn to cook until she was 40. She was 51 years old when she launched her show *The French Chef,* which made her a household name.

- 48-year-old Susan Boyle skyrocketed onto the international stage when she sang on *Britain's Got Talent.* Since then, she has recorded five albums that have sold over 19 million copies and received two Grammy nominations.

> *I am choosing every day to believe that I am worthy and deserving of success, no matter my age or my circumstances.*

Week 6

Leverage The Law of Attraction

AFFIRMATIONS
for
Meditation and Reflection

I am aware that positive actions and emotions attract positive outcomes; I am choosing to radiate positive energy into the Universe and reaping the bounty it reflects back to me.

I am constantly aware of the power of positive thinking and I am supported by the Universe as it brings me endless opportunities for growth.

I am asking for what I want several times a day, believing that I will receive it.

> *What you radiate outward in your*
> *thoughts, feelings, mental pictures, and*
> *words, you attract into your life.*
>
> —CATHERINE PONDER
> Author of *The Dynamic Laws of Prosperity*

Have you ever tried to turn gravity on or off? Probably not because you realize that it can't be done. Well, there's another powerful force in the Universe that—just like gravity—surrounds us and affects us. It's called *The Law of Attraction,* and maybe we can't turn it on or off, but we can harness its tremendous benefits.

To be successful, you must learn how to use The Law of Attraction to create the life you really want. If you're already working on implementing the principles in your life, think of this as a fresh opportunity to brush up on your skills and check your progress. It takes time and consistent effort to train ourselves to behave, think, and speak in only positive ways, but the Universe rewards us exponentially with abundance, joy, and unlimited benefits. Basically, we reap what we sow, and we can freely choose to sow seeds of positivity!

I am aware that positive actions and emotions attract positive outcomes; I am choosing to radiate positive energy into the Universe and reaping the bounty it reflects back to me.

asic chemistry tells us that a physical object, such as a house or a dog or this book, is made up of billions of individual atoms—tiny parcels of energy—that bond together into different forms such as water, metal, and plastic. Similarly, our thoughts are also a form of energy—easily detected as brain waves by standard medical equipment—that can interact with our physical world just like any other form of energy does. When we understand this basic science, we realize that our thoughts can actually *interact with the physical world* and help bring about what we want to happen.

The core tenet of The Law of Attraction says: *What you think about, talk about, believe strongly about, and feel intensely about, you will bring about*. Once you know that, by using your thoughts, you can help bring about the opportunities, resources, and people who can help you accomplish your goals, you'll start paying greater attention to the direction of your thoughts and what you focus on throughout the day.

> *I am constantly aware of the power of positive thinking and I am supported by the Universe as it brings me endless opportunities for growth.*

*E*verything—including you—is vibrating at a specific and unique frequency. That means you can learn to use the power of deliberate thought to stay in a state of higher vibration and attract what you want in life. Here's how:

Step One: Ask for what you want.

Decide what you really want and use words that focus on that goal. Replace negative images and thoughts with positive ones. Consistently ask for what you want and then let the Universe worry about how you'll get it.

Step Two: Believe you'll get what you want, then take action.

Believing means being confident that you've put your future in the hands of a greater power and that your goals can be accomplished. Taking action is another form of belief—after all, we would only take action on goals we believe are possible to begin with.

Step Three: Receive what you want.

One of the best ways to bring yourself into vibrational alignment with what you want is to use affirmations—statements of your goals and desires already achieved in present time. Repeat them regularly so that your subconscious mind maintains a vibrational match to what you want.

*I am asking for what I want several times
a day, believing that I will receive it.*

Week 7

Set Goals That Inspire You

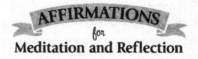

AFFIRMATIONS *for* **Meditation and Reflection**

I am clear about what my goals are and I know that I will accomplish them.

I am visualizing my breakthrough goal as if it's already been accomplished, and I'm feeling the joyful emotions of living the life of my dreams.

I am amazed how far I can go when I set goals and go after them with conviction and confidence.

*If you want to be happy, set a goal that commands your
thoughts, liberates your energy, and inspires your hopes.*

—ANDREW CARNEGIE
American steel industrialist and one of the richest people in history

uccess is not only an attitude and belief system, it's also a
science. Experts on the science of success know that the
brain is a goal-seeking organism, and when you give it a
specific goal, it will work overtime to achieve it.

Dr. Gail Matthews of Dominican University conducted a
study proving that people who write down their goals, then
create action steps to achieve them—and make regular progress reports to a friend—have nearly double the success rate at
achieving what they want! Think about it: by taking a few extra
steps, you can be *twice* as successful as those people who merely
think about their goals.

It may surprise you to also learn that the small percentage
of Americans who write down their goals and regularly review
them earn *nine times more* over the course of their lifetimes than
those who don't.* This alone should motivate you to write down
your goals!

> *I am clear about what my goals are and
> I know that I will accomplish them.*

---

* Statistics from a study by professor emeritus David Kohl of Virginia Polytechnic Institute and State
University.

*I*f you have no criteria for measuring the successful completion of a goal, you don't have a true goal—you simply have a good idea. An actual goal that inspires action and unleashes the power of your subconscious mind must include *how much* (a measurable quantity) and *by when* (a specific time and date for completion).

One of the best ways to get clarity on your goals is to write them out in detail. When you write it all down, your subconscious will know *specifically* what to work on, including which opportunities to focus on to bring about success. Reread your goals three times a day—close your eyes and picture each one as if it were already accomplished and imagine how it feels to actually be living with that achievement.

Most of our goals represent incremental improvements in our life—get new car insurance, clean that closet, finish this week's sales presentation. But, what if you could work toward accomplishing a *breakthrough goal*—something that substantially improves life as you know it, such as buying your first home or starting a business or funding your retirement? Those are the kind of goals that are worth pursuing with passion. Write down a few breakthrough goals for your vision—including a completion date. Then focus on those quantum leaps that will change your life.

> *I am visualizing my breakthrough goal as if it's already been accomplished, and I'm feeling the joyful emotions of living the life of my dreams.*

Once a goal is set, three things will emerge that stop most people—but they're not going to stop you! They are *considerations, fears,* and *roadblocks.*

Let's say you decide to double your income by the end of the year. Before you know it, thoughts will emerge like *I won't have time for my family* or *I'll have to work twice as many hours.* These thoughts are *considerations.* They've been in your subconscious a long time, but now that they have come to light, you can address them and move on.

Fears, on the other hand, are feelings: You may have a fear of rejection, a fear of being laughed at, or a fear of failure. But fears are also just part of the process of moving toward your goals. Knowing that in advance helps you overcome them.

Roadblocks are purely external circumstances that can be overcome such as not having the money to start a new business or needing additional training before seeking a promotion. Roadblocks are obstacles that appear in your path, but they also are just things you will have to deal with.

Once you know to expect considerations, fears, and roadblocks, you'll realize they're not as overwhelming as you thought. Learn to accept and confront them because, more often than not, they are the very things that have been holding you back in life.

I am amazed how far I can go when I set goals and go after them with conviction and confidence.

Week 8

Take a Goal and Chunk It Down

I am comfortable asking for guidance and advice from people who have already done what I want to do.

I am using mind-mapping skills to break down large goals into smaller, manageable tasks and I'm accomplishing them one at a time.

I am planning my day the night before, which allows my subconscious mind to work throughout the night on accomplishing my goals.

The secret of getting ahead is getting started.
The secret of getting started is breaking your complex,
overwhelming tasks into small, manageable tasks,
and then starting on the first one.

—SAMUEL LANGHORNE CLEMENS
Better known as the American writer,
humorist, and entrepreneur Mark Twain

When you break down large goals into small tasks and accomplish them one at a time, you'll move forward much more easily. It's known as "chunking it down." That's how big goals are achieved.

One great way to discover the individual steps is to ask people who have already accomplished what you want to do. From personal experience, they can guide you through the necessary steps and give you advice on how to avoid common pitfalls. You can also purchase books or guides, take online courses, or even start from your end goal and look backward. Imagine that you have already achieved your goal, what did you do to get where you are now? What was the last thing you did? And the thing before that? When you find the first thing you did, that's your starting point.

> *I am comfortable asking for guidance*
> *and advice from people who have already*
> *done what I want to do.*

Mind mapping is a simple yet powerful process for creating a to-do list for achieving your goal. It lets you determine things like who you need to talk to, what information you need to pull together, what the deadlines are that you need to meet, and more. If you've always dreamed of becoming an author and want to write your first book—a breakthrough goal that would lead to an extraordinary new career—you could use mind mapping to help you "chunk down" your very large goal into smaller steps.

Here's how mind mapping* works:

1) Draw a circle in the center of a page. Inside the circle, jot down the name of your major goal *(write a book).*

2) Divide your goal into the major subcategories of tasks you'll need to do to accomplish the primary goal and draw a mini-circle for each *(interview experts, find an agent).*

3) Draw several lines radiating outward from each mini-circle and label each line with its corresponding small task *(write an email asking for an interview, hire a transcriber on* Fiverr.com*).*

4) Break down each one of the small tasks with action items to create a master to-do list.

> *I am using mind-mapping skills to break down large goals into smaller, manageable tasks and I'm accomplishing them one at a time.*

---

* To help you create your own mind map, check out the free resources on my website *www.success principles.com,* or watch my video "Canfield Coaching: Mind Mapping" on YouTube.

Once you've created a mind map for your goal, you'll have to transform all of your to-do items into action items. List each item on your daily to-do list separately, along with a completion date. Transfer them to your calendar and schedule them in the proper order, then do whatever is necessary to stay on track.

We recommend that you plan your day the night before—make a fresh to-do list based on the current day's accomplishments and outcomes. Spend a few minutes visualizing exactly how you want the day to go, and your subconscious mind will work during the night thinking of creative ways to reach the goals you set out to achieve.

Each morning, your plan should be to complete the most important items on your to-do list first. Here's a tip for making this a success: As soon as you take out your list, identify five things you absolutely must accomplish that day, then number them one through five, with one being the item you least enjoy and five being the item you most enjoy. By putting the item you least enjoy at the top of your list, it becomes your first task of the day. Now, not only won't you spend the whole day thinking about it, but getting it done first creates momentum and builds confidence, setting the tone for the rest of the day.

I am planning my day the night before, which allows my subconscious mind to work throughout the night on accomplishing my goals.

Week 9

Success Leaves Clues

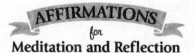

I am seeking out and finding clues left by others that help me achieve my goals.

I am seeking out and working with mentors who can teach me what I need to know to be successful.

I am alert when people speak on topics directly or indirectly related to my goals because they contain valuable clues that I want to learn.

*Long ago, I realized that success leaves clues,
and that people who produce outstanding results do
specific things to create those results. I believed that if
I precisely duplicated the actions of others, I could
reproduce the same quality of results that they had.*

—ANTHONY ROBBINS
Author of *Unlimited Power*

Clues are easy to find if you're willing to look. Almost anything you can think of has already been done by someone else—whether it's losing weight, raising a family, or starting a business—and that's great news because it means they have left clues about how they achieved their success. You can identify these clues and mimic their actions on your own path to reach these same major goals.

For example, if you've just been promoted at the office and want to eventually reach the senior executive level, there are hundreds of books for you to read on the topics of leadership, personal success, goal setting, human psychology, and more. You can also read my other books, *The Success Principles* and *The Power of Focus,* or participate in my *Breakthrough to Success* seminar. What's more, just a phone call away are people who are available as teachers, mentors, advisors, and consultants.

*I am seeking out and finding clues left by
others that help me achieve my goals.*

A couple of years ago I was in Dallas preparing to go on a morning news show and I asked the makeup artist what her long-term goals were. She said she'd always thought about opening her own beauty salon, so I asked her what she was doing to make that happen. "Nothing," she said, "because I don't know how to go about it."

I suggested she offer to take a salon owner to lunch and interview her about how she did it.

"You can do that?" the makeup artist exclaimed.

Absolutely you can—and there are many people within reach who would love to talk about what they do and how they came to be doing it. Whatever your dream is, there is someone who has achieved a similar dream and has clues to share—but you have to make the move and *ask*. You can even offer to volunteer or intern with one of them so that you can get a hands-on learning experience—*talk about finding clues!*

> *I am seeking out and working with mentors who can teach me what I need to know to be successful.*

At some time or another, you've probably thought about asking an expert for advice yourself, but shrugged it off with thoughts such as *Why would someone take the time out of their day to talk with me? Why would they want to potentially create their own competition?* Stop! You're creating roadblocks in your own mind that don't even exist. Most people love to talk about how they built their business or accomplished their goals.

Here are a few reasons why we don't take advantage of this resource that's so readily available:

- We're too reluctant to do something no one else we know is doing.

- We'd have to go out of our way or take time from something else—like friends or hobbies.

- Our fear of rejection overrides our desire to ask for advice or information.

- We'd have to do something different, and even when it's in our own best interest, change is uncomfortable.

- We'd have to work at it, and frankly, most people just don't want to work that hard.

> *I am alert when people speak on topics directly or indirectly related to my goals because they contain valuable clues that I want to learn.*

Week
10

Use Affirmations to Release the Brakes

AFFIRMATIONS
for
Meditation and Reflection

I am "releasing the brakes" by letting go of limiting beliefs and focusing on the certainty of my success.

I am expanding my comfort zone every day by using affirmations that fill my subconscious mind with positive thoughts and images.

I am constantly thinking, talking, and writing about the reality I want to create.

45

*Everything you want is just outside
your comfort zone.*

—ROBERT ALLEN
Bestselling author of *Multiple Streams of Income*

Have you ever driven your car and realized that the emergency brake was on? What did you do to overcome the resistance of the brake? Did you step harder on the gas? No, you probably released the brake and the car accelerated on its own without any extra effort.

We do the same thing in our lives. We hold on to negative images, toxic experiences, and difficult relationships from our past that we haven't processed yet. Sometimes our beliefs about reality are simply incorrect and we harbor guilt and self-doubt because we either don't want or don't know how to let go. No matter how hard we try, the drag from these experiences and emotions cancels out our forward progress when we try to achieve our goals. But we will never be able to get exactly what we want in life unless we release these brakes—and that means letting go of our limiting beliefs, thoughts, and negative emotions like guilt, fear, anger, and resentment.

> *I am "releasing the brakes" by
> letting go of limiting beliefs and focusing
> on the certainty of my success.*

*Y*our comfort zone is basically a self-created prison that you live in, made from a collection of cant's, must's, must nots, and other baseless beliefs created by all the negative thoughts you have allowed to reside in your subconscious mind during your lifetime.

We create an endless loop of responses that reinforce negative or erroneous behaviors, which keep us trapped in our self-made "comfort zone." Constant complaining (as we discussed earlier) focuses our mind on our present circumstances and gets us caught once again in the endless circle of negative self-talk—those cant's, mustn'ts, and so on.

But we can change the cycle. We can focus instead on flooding our minds with positive thoughts, words and images especially through the use of affirmations. These affirmations—and the positive self-talk that they bombard our brain with—actually create new pathways in our subconscious mind and steer us off the hamster wheel—that ingrained cycle of insanity that we've created for ourselves. We are never truly stuck. We can change—and committing to a steady diet of affirmations will get us there!

> *I am expanding my comfort zone every day by using affirmations that fill my subconscious mind with positive thoughts and images.*

Though we've provided a "starter set" of affirmations at the beginning of each chapter in this book, it's up to you to write and begin using affirmations that are specific to your circumstances and life goals. Use the guidelines below to make your personal affirmations powerfully effective:

1) **Start with the words "I am."** Your subconscious mind interprets these two powerful words as a command—they are the most effective words in our language.

2) **Use the present tense.** Describe what you want as though it has already been accomplished.

3) **State it in the positive.** Don't think about what you don't want—affirm what you *do* want.

4) **Keep it brief.** Make it short enough to be easily remembered.

5) **Make it specific.** Vague affirmations produce vague results.

6) **Include an action word ending with** *-ing.* This adds power.

7) **Include at least one dynamic emotion or feeling.** What would you be feeling if you had already achieved the goal?

8) **Make affirmations for yourself, not others.** Don't include someone else's actions. What will *you* be doing?

9) **Add "or something better."** Our experience often limits what we ask for. Always ask for more.

> *I am constantly thinking, talking, and writing about the reality I want to create.*

**Week
11**

See What You Want,
Get What You See

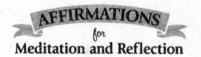

AFFIRMATIONS
for
Meditation and Reflection

*Each night before retiring I am confidently reading
my list of goals out loud and creating images of
the completed goals in my mind.*

*By adding sounds, smells, and feelings to my
internal pictures, I am multiplying the benefits
many times over.*

*I am heightening the impact of my affirmations by
focusing and clearly visualizing them.*

> *Imagination is everything.*
> *It is the preview of life's coming attractions.*
>
> —ALBERT EINSTEIN
> Winner of the Nobel Prize for Physics

Visualization is the technique of closing your eyes and picturing yourself enjoying life as if your goals had already been achieved—in rich, vivid, colorful detail. It's seeing in your mind's eye the places you would be, the sounds you would hear, the emotions you'd be feeling, and the actions you would be taking.

Visualization is one of the most effective tools you can use to reach your goals because it accelerates your success immensely.

- It allows your brain's *reticular activating system* to "let through" ideas, observations, people, and opportunities from amongst the millions of images it processes for you every day.

- Through The Law of Attraction, visualization *attracts to you* the people and opportunities that will benefit you.

When meditating on your affirmations, repeat them aloud and visualize them in vivid Technicolor so they produce clear images in your mind. Be very specific on the details so that your affirmations release the creative powers that fuel success.

> *Each night before retiring I am confidently reading my list of goals out loud and creating images of the completed goals in my mind.*

Before *Chicken Soup for the Soul* ever hit #1, Mark Victor Hansen and I created a mock-up of the *New York Times* Bestsellers List with the book's cover in the #1 spot. Within 15 months, that dream became a reality!

Make the most out of visualizing your affirmations by applying these same principles:

- Add sounds, smells, tastes, and feelings to your images. What does it sound like at your home on the beach? How does the sea smell? What feelings would you be experiencing?

- Use emotions to add fuel to your vision. When confronted with intense emotions, an image or scene can stay locked in our memory forever. Use this phenomenon to its fullest benefit by infusing your visions with emotion and energy!

Most of us don't see things in bright three-dimensional images when we close our eyes; actually, we don't really *see* an image as much as we *think* it. To help you truly see and focus on your goals, find pictures of your dream vacation, you at your perfect weight, a black Tesla P100D, and then glue them to a small poster board. Then display it where you can see it every day. You can also write your personal affirmations on index cards using color felt markers, then draw illustrations of your dream house or perfect job.

> *By adding sounds, smells, and feelings to my internal pictures, I am multiplying the benefits many times over.*

*Y*our brain operates very differently from your physical body. To your brain, there is no difference between visualizing something and actually doing it. Arnold Schwarzenegger, actor, body builder, film producer, and former governor of California, once said, "Create a vision of who you want to be, and then live into that picture as if it were already true." I'd say that strategy worked pretty well for him.

You may not be aware of it, but when you visualize your goals as having already been achieved, your subconscious mind will find a way to turn your current situation into the new vision that you have been feeding it. If you feed your mind pictures of a beautiful home, a loving relationship, and an exciting career, it will work on achieving those things. On the other hand, if you are constantly feeding it negative pictures, like a stressful job, an impossible feat, or a failing relationship—guess what?—it will work to achieve those, too.

Set aside time each and every day to visualize every one of your goals as already complete. This is one of the most vital things you can do to make your dreams come true. Some psychologists say that an hour of visualization is equal to seven hours of physical effort. That's a pretty big claim, but still, imagine what would happen to your life if you did that every day!

I am heightening the impact of my affirmations by focusing and clearly visualizing them.

Week 12

Act As If

AFFIRMATIONS
for
Meditation and Reflection

I am believing and acting as if I am already where I want to be.

I am exuding self-confidence and asking for what I want with complete faith that I will get it.

I am laying down powerful blueprints in my subconscious mind to make my dreams come true.

Believe and act as if it were impossible to fail.

—CHARLES F. KETTERING
Engineer, businessman, and inventor with over 186 patents

One of the greatest strategies for success is to *act as if* you are already where you want to be. That requires you to think, talk, act, dress, and feel like you have already achieved your goals. Acting "as if" projects to the world a sense of confidence and achievement, sending powerful messages to your subconscious mind, which is designed to find unique ways to solve problems. It also programs your brain's *reticular activating system*—the function that allows into your awareness useful information from the millions of pieces of information you process every day—to make you aware of hidden resources that may help you. What's more, when you act as if, The Law of Attraction comes into play, since acting "as if" sends strong vibrations to the Universe that you are committed to achieving your goal—and that you are open to accepting and applying anything it sends your way.

One of my favorite books is *Jonathan Livingston Seagull* by Richard Bach, who writes, "To fly as fast as thought, to be anywhere there is, you must first begin by knowing that you have already arrived." Pretty sound advice and one of life's greatest lessons.

I am believing and acting as if I am already where I want to be.

*Y*ou can begin right now to act as if you've already achieved the goals you set for yourself. Once you start acting successful, that outer experience will create the inner experience—the feelings, emotions, confidence, and thoughts—that will lead you to the fulfillment of your goal.

How would you act if you were already a straight-A student, a bestselling author, an Olympic athlete, a top salesperson, a celebrated musician, or a successful entrepreneur? How would you think, talk, carry yourself, dress, treat other people, handle money, and so forth?

There are a couple of very important lessons we can learn from the behavior of successful people: they exude self-confidence, they've learned the power of asking for what they want, they speak up about what they don't want, they take risks and celebrate their successes, and they also save a portion of their income and share a portion with others.

These are all things that you can start to do right now. They don't cost more money, but they do require intention. And as soon as you start acting "as if," the people and things that will help you achieve your goals in real life will start being drawn to you.

> *I am exuding self-confidence and asking for what I want with complete faith that I will get it.*

*I*t's imperative that you start now being who you want to be—don't let any more time pass while you're "thinking it over." Why? Because inaction is the same as never taking action. Start now and be who you want to be, then do the things that go along with being that person, and soon you'll find that you easily have everything you want in life—health, wealth, fulfilling relationships, and social impact.

Tania Kotsos, author and creator of *Mind Your Reality*, says: "It is your subconscious mind that is the storehouse of your deep-seated beliefs and programs. To change your circumstances and attract to yourself that which you choose, you must learn to program and re-program your subconscious mind."

For thousands of years this principle has been with us and yet so few people actually put it to use. Let those words inspire you into action!

> *I am laying down powerful blueprints*
> *in my subconscious mind to make*
> *my dreams come true.*

Week 13

Take Action, Even If You Don't Know the Whole Path

As I take action, all things are becoming clearer and easier for me because I am constantly attracting people who are encouraging and supporting me.

When I make mistakes, I know there is something valuable that I am learning from each experience.

I am enjoying getting feedback that is helping me make the corrections I need to become successful.

57

> *Things may come to those who wait, but only
> the things left by those who hustle.*
>
> —ABRAHAM LINCOLN
> Sixteenth president of the United States

*I*t's long been known by successful people that the world doesn't reward you for what you know. It rewards you for what you do. Yet, as obvious and practical as that statement is, millions of people every day get tied up analyzing, planning, and organizing instead of simply taking action. They seem to look the other way hoping the rules will change while they're preoccupied.

In the end, however, what we know or what we believe is of little consequence. The only thing that matters is *what you do*.

What happens the day you decide to take action? People will wake up and start paying attention to you. People with similar goals will fall into alignment with you. You will begin learning things from experience. Things that once seemed confusing will become clear, and things that once appeared difficult will become easier. You will attract others who will support and encourage you, and wonderful things will begin to flow toward you—*once you take action*.

> *As I take action, all things are
> becoming clearer and easier for me because
> I am constantly attracting people who
> are encouraging and supporting me.*

There's an exercise that I use in my seminars to demonstrate the power of taking action. I hold up a $100 bill and ask, "Who would like this $100 bill?" Lots of people start waving their hands back and forth. Other people shout out, "I want it!" or "Give it to me!" But I just continue standing there holding up the $100 bill until someone actually gets out of their chair and comes up and takes it out of my hand. When I ask the group how many of them thought about standing up and coming up to take the money but stopped themselves, half the room raises their hands. What did they say to themselves?

"I was sitting too far back in the room."

"I didn't want it to look like I needed it that badly."

"I wasn't sure if you would really give it to me."

"I didn't want to look greedy."

"I was afraid I would be doing something wrong and that people would judge me or laugh at me."

"I was waiting for further instructions."

So, what did the person who actually got the money do that no one else in the room did to end up $100 richer? She got off her butt and took action—she did what was necessary to get the money—and that's exactly what you need to do if you want to be successful!

> *When I make mistakes, I know*
> *there is something valuable that I am*
> *learning from each experience.*

*I*n order to be successful, you have to *do* what successful people do, and successful people are highly action-oriented. If you hold yourself back for fear of looking foolish in one situation, you probably hold yourself back for fear of looking foolish in others. You have to identify those patterns, break through them, and stop holding yourself back.

Most people don't take action because they are afraid of failing. Successful people, on the other hand, realize that failure is an inevitable and natural part of the learning process. They know that failure is just a way that we learn by trial and error.

Once you embrace failure as part of the journey to success, you'll be much more willing to just get started, make mistakes along the way, pay attention to the feedback you receive, make the necessary corrections, and keep moving forward toward your goal. Every experience you have will yield more useful information that you can apply to the next action you take.

So, by now, you have gone through the necessary foundational steps to success—created a vision, set specific and measurable goals, broken them down into small steps, visualized and affirmed your success, and chosen to believe in yourself and your dreams. Now it's time to take action.

> *I am enjoying getting feedback*
> *that is helping me make the corrections*
> *I need to become successful.*

Week 14

Lean into It and See If It Feels Right to You

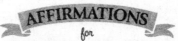

I am leaning into what I want to do and seeing any roadblocks as opportunities to develop new skills, greater confidence, and perseverance.

As I lean into new activities, I am letting God know that I am willing to use my talents to make the world around me a better place.

I am willing to start without seeing the whole path because I believe it will take me where I want to go—or even someplace better.

A journey of 1,000 miles begins with one step.
—ANCIENT CHINESE PROVERB

When someone says something important that will help you, or when someone makes you an offer related to something you want to do, your job is to "lean into it." Dip your toe in the water and see what that opportunity feels like.

Many of the world's most successful people got that way because they paid attention to a door opening in front of them. They had the courage and wisdom to walk through that door and "lean into" the opportunity on the other side. They worked several months on a start-up company. They did a free speaking engagement for a global organization. They spent a few hundred dollars flying across the country to meet a new contact. They checked out the opportunity, learned something new, and determined whether that new path was the one that would lead them to their goal.

Oftentimes, ultimate success finds you when you're leaning into something. That's when you find yourself open to opportunities and willing to do whatever it takes to succeed—without any expectation whatsoever. The time for thinking is over and the time to take action has begun.

> *I am leaning into what I want to do and seeing any roadblocks as opportunities to develop new skills, greater confidence, and perseverance.*

omentum is one of the wonderful outcomes of leaning into it. Momentum begins to build the minute you take your first step toward making your dreams a reality. It's a magnetic force—an energy that attracts people, resources, and opportunities into your life. Just when you need them—at the perfect time when you can most benefit—they will become available to you and doors will open in ways you may not expect. Oftentimes, that's how great things happen—but you have to first prepare the soil in which they can take root, thrive, and grow.

Martin Luther King Jr., the great civil rights leader and Nobel Peace Prize recipient, said, "Take the first step in faith. You don't have to see the whole staircase. Just take the first step."

He realized that sometimes the exact thing you need to propel you further, to help you achieve a breakthrough goal, is just ahead beyond where you can see it. Unless you take that first step forward, you'll never know just how close it is. Have faith. Be willing to take the step and lean into it.

> *As I lean into new activities,*
> *I am letting God know that I am willing*
> *to use my talents to make the world*
> *around me a better place.*

irst you jump off the cliff and you build wings on the way down. Science fiction author Ray Bradbury said that, and it has become one of my favorite quotes. There is no perfect time or situation for you to begin creating and achieving your goals. Don't keep putting things off waiting for a special sign, a double rainbow, or for 12 doves to fly overhead in the sign of a cross.

When Mark Victor Hansen and I first released *Chicken Soup for the Soul*, I thought it would be a good idea to sell the book in bulk to large network marketing companies. I knew those books could motivate their sales force to believe in their dreams, take more risks, and achieve greater success. So, I started cold-calling these companies—something I had never done before. Sometimes I was told they weren't interested, sometimes I got hung up on, but eventually, not only did I make some significant sales, a few of the companies liked the book so much they hired me to speak at their national conventions.

Most of life is on-the-job training and some of the most important things can only be learned in the process of doing them. You have to just start—from wherever you are—in order to get where you want to be.

> ***I am willing to start without seeing the whole path because I believe it will take me where I want to go—or even someplace better.***

**Week
15**

Experience Your Fear and
Take Action Anyway

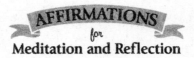

for
Meditation and Reflection

*I am confidently and courageously confronting my
fears and moving forward.*

*I am growing and feeling liberated by doing the
very things I was afraid to do.*

*I am replacing my self-created, imaginary images
and sensations of fear with positive images and
sensations of my desired outcome.*

We come this way but once.
We can either tiptoe through life and hope that
we get to death without being too badly bruised, or
we can live a full, complete life, achieving our
goals and realizing our wildest dreams.

—BOB PROCTOR
Self-made millionaire and featured teacher
in the book and movie, *The Secret*

As you move forward on your journey from where you are to where you want to be, you are going to have to face your fears. Fear is normal. And it keeps you on your toes.

If you are one of those people who run the other way when you feel a pang of fear, be aware that there's something far more scary: never really living the life you want. The truth is, people do lose their footing, they do lose their jobs, they do forget their lines. William G. T. Shedd once said, "A ship is safe in the harbor, but that's not what it's for."

You have already clarified why you're here on this Earth. And you've made a commitment to reach your goals. The only way you will be successful and eventually become who you were meant to be is to leave your safe zone and trust that you will make it.

I am confidently and courageously confronting
my fears and moving forward.

*I*n my book *The Success Principles: How to Get from Where You Are to Where You Want to Be*, I talk about **F.E.A.R.**, which is an acronym for Fantasized Experiences Appearing Real. It's one of the primary reasons we fail to achieve our goals and fail to find true happiness. We make incorrect assumptions about what's required to be successful and then we actually believe these assumptions. Sadly, the limits we put on ourselves because of our erroneous beliefs prevent us from being as happy as we could be, or achieving a great measure of success.

It's important to remember that almost all of your fears are self-created, but once you decide that an idea is true, you attach yourself to it even though it has little or no merit at all. Freeing yourself from your erroneous beliefs can be difficult. Yet, because you are the one doing the fantasizing, you also have the ability to end the fear by facing the real facts and not giving into your negative images.

Here's a little exercise that can help you overcome fear: Write down something you are afraid to do—like asking your boss for a raise. Then, write down why you are afraid to do it—e.g., *I want to ask my boss for a raise, but I keep imagining he will say no and get angry.* See? That kind of fear is not even real—you're imagining a response that may never happen, and you may never get that raise if you don't overcome your self-created fear and ASK!

> *I am growing and feeling liberated by doing the very things I was afraid to do.*

Celebrated American author and humorist Mark Twain once said, "I have lived a long life and had many troubles, most of which never happened."

Think about that. Are you living your life worrying about and avoiding imaginary troubles, many of which actually never happen? We all do that from time to time—some of us more than others. The solution to this problem is to train our internal eyes to recognize the limits we put on ourselves by worrying and entertaining negative thoughts—then deal with them.

Here are four very effective approaches to overcoming unfounded fears:

1) Identify what you're imagining that frightens you, then replace that image with its positive opposite. Write it in the form of an affirmation.
2) Focus on the physical sensations of your fear, then focus on the feelings you would like to be experiencing instead.
3) Remember a time when you triumphed in the face of fear—like giving a speech or passing an important exam.
4) If your fear is so big that it's paralyzing, scale down the risk. Take small steps first, then take on the bigger challenges at a later time.

I am replacing my self-created, imaginary images and sensations of fear with positive images and sensations of my desired outcome.

Week
16

Be Willing to Pay the Price of Success

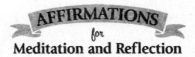
for
Meditation and Reflection

I am willing to pay the price to achieve my goals and dreams on my own terms.

I am doing whatever it takes to be successful and reach my goals.

I am committed to investing the time, money, and effort required to achieve my most important goals.

Practice isn't the thing you do once you're good;
it's the thing you do that makes you good.

—MALCOLM GLADWELL
Author of *Outliers: The Story of Success*
and other bestsellers

Behind every success story there is a tale of perseverance and dedication. In order to be great, it takes a lot of education, training, practice, discipline, and sacrifice. You have to be willing to put in the time and effort—to do what it takes to succeed. That often means a steady diet of trial and error and constant practice—generally in more than one area. But it's the *willingness* to do what's necessary that adds that extra dimension and pushes you past setbacks, challenges, roadblocks, and even emotional and physical pain. I love this quote from the great Bear Bryant (still college football's winningest coach): "It's not the will to win that matters—everyone has that. It's the will to prepare to win that matters."

Preparing to win means doing whatever it takes—getting to work early, taking extra courses, practicing the piano one more hour every day. That's what makes the difference between elite performers and people who are just good at something.

Persevere and you will stand out from the rest.

I am willing to pay the price to achieve my
goals and dreams on my own terms.

*E*ven though today's multitalented, multimillionaire Oprah Winfrey struggled when she was a little girl, she was determined. She believed in herself and honed her skills. Today she's one of the most successful women in the world.

When she was asked what her secret to success was, she said, "The big secret in life is that there is no secret. Whatever is your goal, you can get there if you are willing to work."

Are you willing to do the work you need to do to achieve your goals and dreams? Part of paying the price is the willingness to do whatever it takes to get the job done—no excuses. When M. Scott Peck published *The Road Less Traveled,* he participated in thousands of radio interviews and continued to do one each day for the next 13 years, keeping the book on the *New York Times* bestseller list for 694 weeks. Pulitzer and Nobel prize winner Ernest Hemingway rewrote *A Farewell to Arms* 39 times.

What's more, numerous studies show that practicing toward a specific goal is what helps elite performers overcome a lack of innate talent or prevail over other deficiencies. Imagine what you could achieve if you set a goal and really practiced doing the things that would help you succeed!

> *I am doing whatever it takes to be successful and reach my goals.*

When a SpaceX rocket takes off from Cape Canaveral, it uses up a large portion of its total fuel just to overcome the gravitational pull of the Earth. Once it is free of gravity, it can pretty much glide through space for the rest of its mission. That's the result of building momentum. It's like that in business and careers as well; you have to do what it takes to get to the place where people see you as an expert and a person of integrity. And, as long as you maintain a high level of professionalism, you will be able to reap the benefits for a long time.

One of the key pieces of advice that I constantly give people in my training classes and lectures is *find out the price you have to pay*. How can you decide to pay the price when you have no idea what it costs? You may have to do some investigating—turn over some rocks, make notes, do some research, interview some people—in order to find out what is required for you to succeed (or even just take the first steps). Bear in mind that "cost" can relate to money, health, time, labor, time spent away from family, and more. Once you know what the cost will be, you can decide whether it is still right for you or if there's something better on the horizon. Be aware, be open, and be prepared. God may have something even better in store for you!

> *I am committed to investing the time, money, and effort required to achieve my most important goals.*

Week 17

You've Gotta Ask

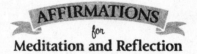

AFFIRMATIONS
for
Meditation and Reflection

I am asking for what I want and need with a positive expectation that I will get a YES.

I am being clear and specific when I ask for something and I'm getting exactly what I want—or something better.

I have both the capacity and tenacity to persevere, so I keep on asking until I succeed.

> *You've got to ask. Asking is, in my opinion,*
> *the world's most powerful and neglected*
> *secret to success and happiness.*

—PERCY ROSS
Self-made multimillionaire
and philanthropist

What's the worst that can happen if you don't have the courage and self-confidence to ask for what you want? For one, you'll never get it, and two, you may be blocking the very thing that will lead to your ultimate success. And if you do ask? You'll get a yes or a no. A no just means that wasn't the right door and you must continue to knock until the right door opens. A yes, on the other hand—well, that's what you get when you ask the right people and you ask enough times.

Asking is one of the most powerful success principles of all, yet it's still a challenge that holds most people back.

Here's an important point to remember when you are asking for what you want. Sometimes what we think we want isn't the best thing for us; sometimes we need to reevaluate what we are asking for and why. And sometimes, because we are asking in faith that we will receive it, we get more than we asked for—we get something better.

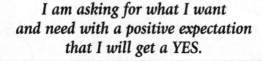

> *I am asking for what I want*
> *and need with a positive expectation*
> *that I will get a YES.*

There's a science for asking for what you want or need in life. Mark Victor Hansen and I have written a whole book about it called *The Aladdin Factor*. Here are some quick tips from the book to get you started.

- **Ask as if you expect to get it.** Ask with the positive expectation that you have already been given it—like it's a done deal.
- **Assume you can.** Don't ever assume against yourself.
- **Ask someone who can give it to you.** Research who that is.
- **Be clear and specific.** When it comes to money, ask for a definite amount. When it comes to requesting a specific behavior, say exactly what you want the person to do.
- **Ask repeatedly.** One of the most important principles of success is persistence. When you're asking others to participate in the fulfillment of your goals, some people are going to say no. More than likely, they have very good reasons for declining. It's not a reflection on you.
- **Don't assume you'll get a no when you haven't even asked yet.** That's rejecting yourself before anyone else has even had a chance. Take the risk—if you get a no, nothing has changed and you are no worse off than before. And you might just get a yes!

I am being clear and specific when I ask for something and I'm getting exactly what I want—or something better.

*L*et's do a little exercise to get you more comfortable with asking for what you want.

Make a list of all the things you want but you haven't asked for—include things relative to home, work, or anywhere else you can think of. Beside each one, write down why you haven't asked for it—what's holding you back? Then write down what you're missing out on by not asking (a good night's sleep, extra time with your family, a promotion). Then, write down the benefits you would gain if you did ask (emotional support, financial gain, help with the housework). Now, do that exercise for everything in the following categories in *Week 3: Decide What You Want to Be, Do, and Have*:

- Your Finances
- Your Job and Career
- Fun Time and Recreation
- Your Health and Fitness
- Your Relationships
- Hobbies and Personal Time
- Your Contributions to the Community

I get that sometimes people are afraid of looking needy or looking foolish, but mostly they are simply afraid of rejection—they are afraid of hearing the word "no." Stop taking it so personally. You need to have not only the capacity, but the tenacity. To be successful, you have to ask!

I have both the capacity and tenacity to persevere, so I keep on asking until I succeed.

Week 18

Don't Let Rejection Stop You

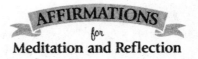

AFFIRMATIONS
for
Meditation and Reflection

I am asking with confidence, knowing that rejection is a myth and only exists in my mind.

I am persevering until I achieve my goals—or something better—because I know that what I want also wants me.

When someone says no to me, rather than getting discouraged, I move on knowing that someone else is waiting to say yes.

We keep going back stronger, not weaker,
because we will not allow rejection to beat us down.
It will only strengthen our resolve.
To be successful, there is no other way.

—EARL G. GRAVES
Founder and publisher of
Black Enterprise magazine

O n your way to becoming successful, you're going to encounter rejection somewhere along the line—it's just a natural part of life. Your application might be denied, you might not be picked for the team, or you might not get the job.

To overcome rejection and keep moving forward, you have to see rejection for what it really is—a myth. When your application isn't accepted or you're not picked for the team, you actually aren't any worse off than before you asked. Nothing has changed, nothing's been taken away from you. You didn't have that $50,000 line of credit before you asked the bank for it, and you don't have it now.

So instead of feeling sad and rejected, ask why you were turned down, hone your proposal, and move on to ask other financial institutions. The reality is, you lose nothing by asking; all you have is something to potentially gain.

I am asking with confidence,
knowing that rejection is a myth and
only exists in my mind.

Today, make a point to accept the idea that you are going to encounter rejection along the way to success. Train your mind to translate the word "no" into "next!" When Colonel Harland Sanders left home with his pressure cooker and his special recipe for Southern fried chicken, he received 1,009 rejections before he found someone to believe in his dream. Because he rejected rejection over 1,000 times, there are now over 19,000 KFC locations in more than 100 countries and territories worldwide.

Maybe his story will help you think about rejection on a smaller scale. It may take a little longer to get what you want, but sometimes the Universe has different (or better) plans for you. In the final analysis, you're really no worse off than before you asked. Don't give up or sulk. Simply find another opportunity.

My *Chicken Soup for the Soul* coauthor Mark Victor Hansen is fond of saying, "What you want wants you." Reject rejection and go for it.

> *I am persevering until I achieve my goals—*
> *or something better—because I know*
> *that what I want also wants me.*

*I*n the fall of 1991, Mark Victor Hansen and I began the progress of selling our first *Chicken Soup for the Soul* book to a publisher. We flew to New York and met with every major publisher that would see us. None of them were interested. We heard rejections like, "Collections of short stories don't sell," and "The title will never work." After that, we were rejected by another 20 publishers who had received the manuscript through the mail. Over 30 rejections later, our agent gave the book back to us because he just couldn't sell it. So, we said, "*Next!*"

The following spring, Mark and I attended the American Booksellers Association convention in Anaheim, California, and walked from booth to booth, talking to anyone who would listen. We were turned down again and again. Still we said, "*Next!*"

At the end of the second very long day, Peter Vegso and Gary Seidler, owners of Health Communications, Inc., a publisher of addiction and recovery books, agreed to look it over. They loved it. Those hundreds of "nexts" finally paid off. After more than 140 rejections, that first book went on to sell over 10 million copies and spawned a series of 250 unique titles. Those titles have been translated into 43 languages with worldwide sales of over 500 million copies! My advice to you? Believe you will succeed and learn to say, "*Next!*"

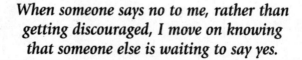

When someone says no to me, rather than getting discouraged, I move on knowing that someone else is waiting to say yes.

Week 19

Listen to Feedback and Use It to Your Advantage

I am welcoming, appreciating, and using the feedback I get, and I accept it as a valuable gift.

I am openly listening to feedback, while at the same time listening to what my body, my feelings, and my instincts are telling me.

I am happily adjusting my behavior and moving forward as I apply the feedback I get from others.

Feedback is the breakfast of champions.

—KEN BLANCHARD AND SPENCER JOHNSON
Coauthors of *The One Minute Manager*

*I*t's human nature to want only positive feedback from others, but there's also great value in constructive negative feedback that can be crucial to your success.

Positive feedback comes in the form of things that make you happy: a raise or promotion at work, surpassing your sales quota, finding balance and inner peace, a loving touch, or making the bestseller list. These things not only make you happy, but they indicate that you are on the right course and making progress.

Negative feedback, on the other hand, comes in the form of things that make you *unhappy:* being broke, conflict at home, an unexpected breakup, loss of a job, and inner discord. But these things hold value for you, too, if you heed them and are willing to make adjustments in your thinking and your behavior. Maybe you missed a turn in the road somewhere, or you veered offtrack. In order for you to be successful, you'll have to learn to pay attention and respond appropriately to *all* the feedback in your life—both positive and negative—because it will teach you what you are doing right, what you are doing wrong, and what changes you need to make.

> *I am welcoming, appreciating, and using the feedback I get, and I accept it as a valuable gift.*

*L*et's talk today about the value of verbal and nonverbal feedback, keeping in mind what we already learned about positive and negative feedback.

Nonverbal feedback comes through body language, actions and attitudes. Have you ever been to a baseball game and by the 7th inning the place has cleared out? That's feedback in action—the fans are saying that they're more interested in avoiding traffic than watching their home team lose. Here's a less obvious example: Have you ever closed a big sale only to find out your new customer placed his next order with a competitor? That's nonverbal feedback telling you that something's wrong. (It should also be telling you to pick up the phone and find out what happened.)

Verbal feedback comes in the form of others talking to you. Let's say you're late again for a meeting and your boss reprimands you in front of your coworkers. That's some serious feedback that's coming in "loud and clear."

But the best type of verbal feedback is the kind you initiate yourself: when you ask your boss about the quality of your work, when you ask your customer what you can do to make his job easier, when you ask your spouse how you can be more attentive or helpful around the house. Seems like a no-brainer, right? Make a commitment today to listen—and respond—to all types of feedback: positive, negative, internal, and external.

> *I am openly listening to feedback, while at the same time listening to what my body, my feelings, and my instincts are telling me.*

*L*et's look at some of the unproductive ways we respond to feedback.

- **Giving Up:** Feedback is simply information—consider it corrective instead of critical and don't take it so personally. Think of it as a caution sign, not a stop sign.

- **Getting mad:** Surely you can recall times when you turned hostile toward someone who gave you feedback that you didn't like. Don't miss out on a relationship and useful information because you don't like what you hear.

- **Ignoring the feedback:** You know those people who don't listen to any point of view unless it conforms to their own? Don't be like them. Feedback could significantly transform your life if you would only listen and respond.

Finally, keep two other points in mind—especially if you're trying to create a winning product, relationship, or service.

- **Some feedback is just wrong.** Is the person giving it to you angry, resentful, egotistical, or vengeful? Be sure that the person giving you the feedback has your best interest at heart.

- **Is there a pattern?** If other people are giving you the same feedback, don't ignore it. Give up your need to be right and listen to legitimate feedback.

> *I am happily adjusting my behavior and moving forward as I apply the feedback I get from others.*

Week
20

Practice Constant and Never-Ending Improvement

AFFIRMATIONS
for
Meditation and Reflection

I am pursuing constant and continuous improvement as I consistently ask myself, How can I make things better and do things with greater love?

I am learning something new and getting more proficient every day, which allows me to pursue even bigger goals in the future.

I am steadily achieving small, manageable steps on the road to my loftiest goals.

We have an innate desire to endlessly learn,
grow, and develop. . . . Once we yield to this inclination for
continuous and never-ending improvement, we lead a
life of endless accomplishments and satisfaction.

—CHUCK GALLOZZI
Author of *The 3 Thieves and 4 Pillars of Happiness*

*I*f you want to be more successful, ask yourself: *How can I make this better? How can I do it more efficiently? How can I do it more profitably? How can I provide more value to more people?* And, equally important: *How can I do it with more love?*

Most industries—perhaps yours—are changing at lightning speed. Technology and information is, too. High-school seniors have never known a time when there were no smartphones or internet. You don't have to become an IT guru, but you do have to keep pace.

It's the same with your profession and your personal finances. Are you keeping up your skills? If you're a parent, what new ways have been discovered for you to raise amazing kids and successfully prepare them for adulthood? Your only intelligent response is to commit to constant improvement—for your career, your health, your family, and your finances.

> *I am pursuing constant and continuous*
> *improvement as I consistently ask myself,*
> *How can I make things better and*
> *do things with greater love?*

*N*ow that we've established that continuous learning is one of the keys to being successful, don't limit your education to just technology or the field you work in. Continuous learning can bring personal improvement, too, like better relationships with your spouse and kids, better health, or learning a new hobby.

Professionally, never-ending improvement might mean upgrading your customer service program, the quality of your product, your online marketing strategy, your sales skills, or your team-building skills. You could also focus on improving your health and fitness, your ability to manage money, or your interpersonal skills. You could also take advantage of the millions of online resources that can help you attain greater inner peace through meditation, yoga, and prayer.

The point is, keep learning, keep growing, and keep improving. It's good for your self-esteem and it's good for your soul—which means it's also good for all your relationships, professional and personal.

> *I am learning something new and getting more proficient every day, which allows me to pursue even bigger goals in the future.*

Today, as you set out to improve your skills, change your behavior, or better your family or business life, consider starting in small, manageable increments to give you a greater chance of long-term success. Doing too much too fast can overwhelm you or even push you into failure. Instead, chunk it down. Start with small steps, master them, and then move on to bigger challenges. It will boost your self-confidence and renew your commitment to succeed. Here are two points to remember:

1) *You can't skip steps.* In our drive-through society, we've come to expect instant gratification—but to become a master at something will take time to develop the depth and breadth of experience that produces expertise, insight, and wisdom.

2) *Apply the power of the slight edge.* In *The Slight Edge*, Jeff Olson talks about the compound effect of doing just a little bit more or a little bit less of something each day—altering your daily habits with a few more push-ups, a little longer meditation, a little more sleep, one less glass of wine, or one less hour of TV. Could you use that time to focus on writing your book, making more sales calls, reading, exercising, doing yoga, meditating, or deepening your relationships?

> *I am steadily achieving small, manageable steps on the road to my loftiest goals.*

Week 21

What Gets Measured Gets Improved

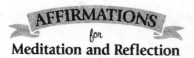
I am consistently posting my target goals and updated scores where I can see them, which motivates me to stay on track.

I am enthusiastically keeping score of my progress, positive behavior changes, financial gains, and the other things I want more of.

I am keeping my life in balance by keeping score of the time I devote to my work, family, health, recreation, community, and spiritual goals.

If you can't measure it, you can't improve it.

—PETER DRUCKER
Management consultant, educator, and author

Remember when you were a first-grader and your teacher gave you stars for projects you did well and for getting to class on time? Do you remember the report card you brought home to show your mom and dad how fast you were learning? You even brought your best projects home to put on the fridge.

Well, nothing's really changed since we were young—we still love to track our success and see progress—except now we can track things like positive behavior, financial gains, and goals achieved. It may not be as visually obvious as a drawing on your fridge, but it still lets you know how you stand in relation to the past and to your future goals. Just like when you were six years old, you still have that natural enthusiasm to keep track of—and improve—your score.

Make a point today to keep score on things that would advance your personal and professional goals the most. Post your scores where you can easily see them to keep you accountable and motivated.

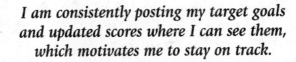

I am consistently posting my target goals and updated scores where I can see them, which motivates me to stay on track.

As a young child, you probably kept score of things that were valuable to you—the number of marbles you collected, the length of time you could hold your breath under water, and the number of goals you scored in soccer. You kept track of things you were good at, things you were proud of, and things you wanted to achieve more of.

It's not much different in business or your profession. You want to develop benchmarks—and exceed them—because they represent a boost in profits and market share or an improvement in your professional capacity. Those benchmarks are called targets or *critical drivers*. To create those targets and track your progress, you will need a checklist of goals you want to reach.

For example: If you're in wealth management, a critical driver may be the percentage of profits you make on assets under management. For a health spa, it might be the number of upsells you make per customer. If you're a handyman, it might be the number of repeat customers you have. Be 100% sure of what your critical drivers are because they are the keys to keeping you continually inspired, motivated, and empowered to meet or beat your targets.

> *I am enthusiastically keeping score*
> *of my progress, positive behavior changes,*
> *financial gains, and the other*
> *things I want more of.*

O f course, scorekeeping isn't just for business or your career, it's for your personal life, too.

If you've been working 60 hours a week—then weekends, too—you might want to look at the impact of that on your family relationships, your health, and your time available to live a balanced, holistic life. Can you keep score in these areas to ensure you improve? Of course you can.

Vinod Khosla, founding CEO of Sun Microsystems and legendary Silicon Valley investor, admitted that when his kids were younger, he kept track of how many times he got home in time to have dinner with them. Simply *saying* you want to spend more time with your family isn't enough—you have to make the effort to *actually do it*. Keeping score will keep you on track.

In fact, if you want to be a high achiever and be successful in every area, you need to determine your goals for your personal life, family time, spiritual journey, health, and wellness—and giving back to community, society, and humanity. Set the goals, create a plan for reaching them, then keep score of your progress in all these other areas. It's that critical.

> *I am keeping my life in balance*
> *by keeping score of the time I devote to*
> *my work, family, health, recreation,*
> *community, and spiritual goals.*

Week
22

Be Persistent

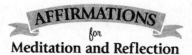

AFFIRMATIONS
for
Meditation and Reflection

I am practicing persistence in pursuing my goals every day because I understand that it's one of the primary qualities of successful people.

I am achieving my goals by following my heart, practicing my daily disciplines, and staying focused on my hopes and dreams.

I am confidently seeking alternative paths of action when needed, knowing that obstacles and roadblocks to my goals can easily be overcome.

*History has demonstrated that the most
notable winners usually encountered heartbreaking
obstacles before they triumphed. They won because they
refused to become discouraged by their defeats.*

—B. C. FORBES
Founder of *Forbes* magazine

istory is overflowing with examples of the virtues of persistence. The most notable winners throughout the ages would have encountered untold challenges before their victories, yet they refused to be defeated.

Take some motivation to always practice persistence from these successful people:

- Henry Ford's early businesses failed and left him broke five times before he founded Ford Motor Company.
- Walt Disney went bankrupt after failing at several businesses. He was even fired from a newspaper for lacking imagination and good ideas.
- Lucille Ball was regarded as a failed actress before she won four Emmys and the Kennedy Center Honors Lifetime Achievement Award.

Being persistent when you encounter obstacles and roadblocks is a requirement for success, and an important source of growth and prosperity.

*I am practicing persistence in pursuing my goals
every day because I understand that it's one of
the primary qualities of successful people.*

There's a big difference between being persistent and just being busy, and the sooner you realize it the better off you'll be. You have already created a plan for each of your goals that outlines the steps you need to take to be successful. Sometimes, your dedication and persistence can get you so engrossed in day-to-day activities that your overarching goal gets buried beneath all the smaller steps you are taking. Don't let busyness cloud your focus on the big picture—your ultimate goal.

If you're spending time filling the hours instead of fulfilling your dreams, you're not maximizing your potential. Remember that The Law of Attraction rewards positive, productive energy with even more positive, productive energy. Don't put limits on your potential to receive abundance, health, opportunity, happiness, and contentment. You are going to need those benefits to get you through any roadblocks and any unforeseen challenges you may face.

Brian Adams, author of *How to Succeed*, wrote, "Difficulties are opportunities to better things; they are stepping stones to greater experience. . . . When one door closes, another always opens; as a natural law it has to, to balance."

I am achieving my goals by following my heart, practicing my daily disciplines, and staying focused on my hopes and dreams.

*C*onsider a few more people totally dedicated to success through persistence:

- **Admiral Robert Peary:** Peary attempted to reach the North Pole seven times before he finally made it on his eighth attempt.
- **Thomas Edison:** It took Edison 1,000 attempts before inventing the lightbulb.
- **Oscar Hammerstein:** This Broadway genius wrote five shows that flopped before hitting pay-dirt with *Oklahoma!*, which ran for 269 weeks and grossed $7 million.

If you are solution oriented in your thinking, you will overcome any obstacle in your path. Here's a tip that will help you: When you encounter an obstacle, find at least three solutions to your problem, then evaluate them carefully one by one. Choose a path that offers the best solution *and persist!*

> *I am confidently seeking alternative paths of action when needed, knowing that obstacles and roadblocks to my goals can easily be overcome.*

Week
23

Learn The Rule of 5

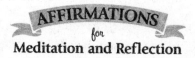

AFFIRMATIONS
for
Meditation and Reflection

I'm enthusiastically reviewing my breakthrough
 goal every day and completing five specific
 actions that are swiftly moving me toward
 achieving that goal.

I am being persistent and consistent, practicing
 The Rule of 5 every single day.

I am being rewarded with a feeling of accomplishment and determination as I work through my
 five daily commitments.

> *Success is the sum of small efforts,*
> *repeated day in and day out.*
>
> —ROBERT COLLIER
> Bestselling author and publisher of *The Secret of the Ages*

When Mark Victor Hansen and I published the first *Chicken Soup for the Soul* book, we were so eager and committed to making it a bestseller that we asked 15 bestselling nonfiction authors for their advice. We visited with a book publishing and marketing guru who gave us even more great information. We read John Kremer's *1001 Ways to Market Your Book*.

We also sought the advice of a wonderful teacher, Ron Scolastico, who told us, "If you would go every day to a very large tree and take five swings at it with a very sharp ax, eventually, no matter how large the tree, it would have to come down." That made a lot of sense and it led us to develop The Rule of 5. The Rule of 5 simply means that every day you do five specific things that will move you forward toward achieving your goal. I challenge you to do the same—commit to doing five things every day that will bring you closer to achieving success.

I'm enthusiastically reviewing my breakthrough goal every day and completing five specific actions that are swiftly moving me toward achieving that goal.

With the goal of getting *Chicken Soup for the Soul* to the top of the *New York Times* bestsellers list, we implemented The Rule of 5 every day, doing things such as giving five radio interviews or sending out five books to reviewers or asking five network marketing companies to buy the book as a motivational tool for their sales people or giving a seminar to at least five people and selling the book at the back of the room. On some days, we would simply send out five free copies to people listed in the *Celebrity Address Book*—radio deejays and talk show hosts, television and movie stars, directors, and producers.

We made phone calls, wrote press releases, called in to talk shows, gave out free copies at our talks, did free talks at churches. We did book signings at every bookstore that would have us, visited gift shops and card shops—we even got gas stations, bakeries, and restaurants to carry the book. It was a lot of effort, but once we chunked down our goals into smaller action steps and persisted every single day, it paid off handsomely.

You know what? About one year from the day it was published, *Chicken Soup for the Soul* finally made it onto a bestseller list. One action at a time, one book at a time, one reader at a time, the sustained effort of The Rule of 5 led to success!

Think you can't do it? Of course you can—anyone can do five things a day if they're focused on a goal!

> *I am being persistent and consistent,*
> *practicing The Rule of 5 every single day.*

*Y*ou have to create your *own* success story using The Rule of 5. No one else can determine your dreams and goals but you—and you will never find fulfillment or contentment trying to pursue someone else's dreams.

Take a look at the list of goals that you created. What five things can you do each and every day to move closer to achieving them? If your goal is to get a raise or a promotion, you could get in early, dress the part, go the extra mile to make your customers happy, exceed your boss's expectations, and so forth. If your goal is to get out of the rat race and buy a cottage by the sea, you could reduce expenses and increase savings, update your current home in order to sell it at a higher price, seek out a real estate agent who can find you great property deals, and create ways to increase your current income.

So, what are your goals—especially your breakthrough goal? Add The Rule of 5 to your daily routine and I promise you will get there faster!

> *I am being rewarded with a feeling of accomplishment and determination as I work through my five daily commitments.*

Week 24

Exceed Expectations in Everything You Do

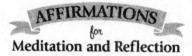

AFFIRMATIONS
for
Meditation and Reflection

I am standing above the crowd by exceeding expectations and overdelivering on my promises.

I am enjoying the personal satisfaction and the financial rewards from choosing to go the extra mile.

I am putting in a little extra effort and providing a little more service, which makes other people happy and me more successful.

It's never crowded along the extra mile.

—WAYNE DYER
Coauthor of *How to Get What You Really,
Really, Really, Really Want*

How many times have you heard someone say, "That's not in my job description," or "That's not what I'm paid to do"? How many people do you know who watch the clock and at five minutes to five o'clock, their computer is off and their keys are in hand?

High achievers know that exceeding expectations makes them stand out from the crowd. They can be counted on when it's crunch time, when someone is short-handed, or when there's a special project that requires above-average attention. They're known as someone who is reliable, who will get the job done well, and who meets a deadline. Successful people simply do more—they exceed expectations. And the payoff is so worthwhile—they will eventually experience far greater financial rewards and immediately begin to experience a personal transformation that manifests as increased self-confidence and greater influence. Even better—they develop a deep feeling of satisfaction and fulfillment at the end of the day!

> *I am standing above the crowd by exceeding expectations and overdelivering on my promises.*

*Y*ou can choose to be a phenomenal success and excel at what you do because exceeding expectations and going the extra mile is actually a choice.

There's a common mind-set today that doing more than you are paid to do isn't good for the rest of the team—maybe management will begin to take it for granted, or maybe when one person steps up it will make the others look bad by comparison. One of the primary problems today facing office culture (and other cultures, too) is that people just don't want to work harder—it's all about them. They believe that working a little longer is unfair, that putting limits on expense accounts means they are not trusted, and that having a dress code is an infringement on their personal style and creativity. But that kind of self-centered individualistic thinking often creates a backlash. They are not a first choice for promotion, they haven't proved that they have much loyalty or integrity, nor have they developed much influence, which excludes them from key planning and brainstorming sessions. That "me only" thinking isn't getting them any brownie points or winning them any awards, either.

One of your greatest assets is your reputation, and going the extra mile won't go unnoticed—by your current employer or by others who will provide new opportunities for you to grow.

> *I am enjoying the personal satisfaction and the financial rewards from choosing to go the extra mile.*

When you exceed expectations, you will experience great personal and professional payoffs, but so will your community, company, colleagues, or family— everyone wins and everyone moves forward together.

Where could you exceed expectations and go the extra mile outside of the workplace or your business? In today's world, it often seems that people are just too busy to help a neighbor with small repairs or pick up an empty soda bottle at the park or hold the door for an elderly person. Long gone, too, are the days when people gave up their seat for a mother and baby or helped someone with a cane to cross the street. These random acts of kindness come from the heart and from your sense of selflessness and generosity. They, too, are examples of going the extra mile in ways that brighten someone else's day—and it doesn't cost you anything to do so.

Plus, you get rewarded, too, since a National Institutes of Health study showed that giving of yourself activates regions of the brain associated with pleasure, social connection, and trust—creating a "warm glow" effect. Scientists also believe that altruistic behavior releases endorphins in the brain, producing the positive feeling known as the "helper's high."*

What can *you* do to go the extra mile for others? *Surprise them and give more than they expect!*

> **I am putting in a little extra effort and providing a little more service, which makes other people happy and me more successful.**

---

* As reported in *Greater Good Magazine*, published by the University of California Berkeley.

Week
25

Surround Yourself with Successful People

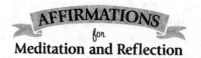

I am joyfully surrounding myself with positive people who have a solution-oriented approach to life.

Because we become like the people we spend the most time with, I am spending my time with people who lift others up rather than put them down.

I am feeling energized being surrounded by people who are happy and committed to lifelong learning.

> *You are the average of the five people*
> *you spend the most time with.*
>
> —JIM ROHN
> Business philosopher and bestselling author

hen I was a first-year history teacher in a Chicago high school, I dubbed the teacher's lounge the "Ain't It Awful Club." Clouds of cigarette smoke and emotional negativity hung constantly in the air. It didn't take long before I was sick and tired of hearing things like, "There is no way you can teach these kids; they are totally out of control." A constant stream of negative judgments, criticisms, blaming, and complaining flowed unabated throughout the lounge.

But by dropping out of the Ain't It Awful Club—by never hanging out in the teacher's lounge—here's how that first year turned out: *I was selected by the students as Teacher of the Year, and it was only my first year of teaching!* I had instead joined a group of dedicated teachers in the school library who actually believed they could overcome any obstacle in their path. I wanted to be successful, and I wanted my students to be successful, so I chose to become a conduit for positivity and encouragement. You can make that choice, too.

> *I am joyfully surrounding*
> *myself with positive people who have a*
> *solution-oriented approach to life.*

Parents are forever telling their children not to associate with certain kids because they know we become like the people we hang out with. If you want to be successful, follow the average parent's advice and start hanging out with successful people.

The other day I ran into a friend who started to tell me how difficult it is for her to meet successful, unmarried men. When I asked her where she'd been looking, she rattled off a list of local bars and nightclubs. I suggested she change her approach and start looking where quality single guys are more likely to hang out.

So it is with friends and anyone else you associate with.

Get active in your industry associations, attend professional conferences and lectures, sign up for a retreat, get active in your Chamber of Commerce or with other civic groups like Toastmasters, Optimists International, and the Rotary Club. Volunteer to serve at your church, temple, or mosque with other leaders. Get on the board of a local charity you care about. When you fly, upgrade to first-class or business-class whenever you can, and use airline premier clubs when you have a layover at the airport. There are lots of places where you'll find high achievers. Go to where *they* are and make some connections.

> *Because we become like the people we spend the most time with, I am spending my time with people who lift others up rather than put them down.*

y mentor W. Clement Stone taught me a valuable exercise that I'd like you to do today:

Make a list of all the people you spend time with regularly, like your family members, colleagues, gym partners, or the people in your church or civic groups. Then, put a minus sign (–) next to the people who are negative and toxic, and put a plus sign (+) next to those who are positive and nurturing.

Do you see a pattern emerging? Is your family or workplace full of toxic people? Are your friends encouraging you or are they triggering a lack of self-esteem and undermining your self-confidence? Make an honest decision about each person on your list based solely on their negative or positive impact on your life.

Now comes the hard part. See all those people in the negative column? Find a way to remove yourself from their sphere of influence or at least reduce the amount of time you spend around them. Try to replace them with people who would fit into the positive column—or spend more time with the positive people already in your life. Until you reach the point in your self-development where you no longer allow people to affect you with their negativity, you're better off spending time alone, doing things like visualizing your dreams!

> *I am feeling energized being surrounded by people who are happy and committed to lifelong learning.*

Week 26

Acknowledge Your
Positive Past

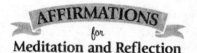

AFFIRMATIONS
for
Meditation and Reflection

I am happily celebrating both my big successes and my small successes.

I am rewarding myself whenever I achieve a goal— encouraging my subconscious mind to create and attract even more success in my life.

I am feeling a great sense of accomplishment, completion, and fulfillment with every goal I achieve.

109

> *I look back on my life like a good day's work;*
> *it is done and I am satisfied with it.*
>
> —GRANDMA MOSES
> One of America's most famous folk artists,
> who only began painting in earnest at age 78

Today, we're going to learn to change the way we view our past failures—and discover the true value of our past successes.

A few chapters back we talked about how the brain is wired to remember past events that were accompanied by strong emotions and sensory stimuli (smell, sound, taste, sight, touch). Most of us underestimate the number of successes we've had because, over time, our brains have been conditioned to remember our failures.

Most people can more easily name 10 failures they've experienced over the past week than 10 successes they've achieved. One of the reasons for this phenomenon is that our standard for labeling something a failure is so low compared to the bar we hold over our heads when determining a success. With affirmations that help you celebrate even "small" successes, you'll be retraining your brain to remember the times you were competent, skillful, insightful, hard-working, and successful.

> *I am happily celebrating both my big*
> *successes and my small successes.*

cknowledging your positive past is important because of the effect it has on your self-esteem. Let's say that you and I are playing poker—you have 10 chips, and I have 200. Lose one or two bets and you're out, while I would be able to continue playing full out—40 times longer, in fact!

Self-esteem is like that—the more you have, the more risks you can take and the longer you can stay in the game.

If your self-esteem is high, you can actually fail at something and it won't destroy you. You would simply dust yourself off, and say, *Next!*—immediately moving forward with a different approach or onto another opportunity altogether.

To help your brain focus on those times you've been successful, here's an exercise I frequently teach:

Divide your life into three time periods (such as 0–15, 16–30, and 31–45 years old, and so on.) Then list three successes for each time period. Better yet, make a list of 100 or more successes you've achieved during your lifetime. Post these lists where you can read them anytime your self-esteem starts to slip a little.

> *I am rewarding myself whenever I achieve a goal—encouraging my subconscious mind to create and attract even more success in my life.*

*L*et's look at some other ways to acknowledge your positive past. Each one is uniquely effective, so I encourage you to give each of them a chance to work in your life.

- **Create a victory log:** Keep a running record of your daily successes. At the end of the day you will be surprised at the number of entries you have. At the end of the week you will be stunned. By the end of the month you will be ecstatic!

- **Display your success symbols:** Whether it's a trophy from Little League, an award from Toastmasters, or a framed copy of your first industry recognition, keep symbols of success where you can see them.

- **Do "The Mirror Exercise":** Uncomfortable, yes, but it will help you give yourself the acknowledgment you deserve—*from yourself.* Stand in front of a mirror, look yourself in the eye, address yourself by name, and appreciate yourself out loud for all the things you've accomplished that day: professional achievements, resolutions you kept, and temptations you avoided. Do it every night before you go to bed for at least 40 days.

> *I am feeling a great sense of accomplishment, completion, and fulfillment with every goal I achieve.*

Week 27

Keep Your Eye on the Prize

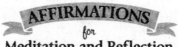

AFFIRMATIONS
for
Meditation and Reflection

I am keeping my thoughts focused on the steps required to reach my goals.

I am giving my full attention to this current moment in my life.

As I sit and quietly contemplate my day, I am bringing more focus and awareness to my mind with every breath I take.

> *Natural ability is important, but*
> *you can go far without it if you have the focus,*
> *drive, desire, and positive attitude.*
>
> —KIRSTEN SWEETLAND
> Canadian Triathlon competitor at the 2016 Olympic Games in Rio de Janeiro

Have you ever noticed that successful people just seem to be more positive? They're focused on their goals, they're possibility thinkers, and they expect positive outcomes when they take action.

You, too, can keep your eye on the prize.

The first step is to determine your most important goals—those that will amplify your life and change who you are as a person, as well as goals that will involve you in exciting new projects and personal connections. The second step is to break those goals down into "baby steps"—individual tasks that will slowly and steadily get you to your goal. Once you know the steps, you can eliminate distractions to focus solely on those steps.

If your goal, for instance, is to start your own small business, your checklist of steps might include researching your industry, creating a budget, acquiring financing, building your personal savings, researching vendors to supply products, and finding subcontractors who can help you deliver services and market the business. Whatever your goal, list the steps you'd need to take—in great detail—so you know what to focus on each day.

> *I am keeping my thoughts focused on the*
> *steps required to reach my goals.*

I like 3x5 note cards. In fact, I carry a stack of them in my pocket and write down ideas that come to me about ways I can achieve my goals. They help me stay focused.

You, too, can create the habit of staying focused on the end game with a list of daily tasks or milestones to accomplish. Tim Ferriss, author of *The Four-Hour Workweek* and numerous other blockbuster bestsellers, calls these tasks "MITs"—most important tasks. And whether you use your smartphone or day planner or an app on your desktop computer, realize that this kind of intense focus and constant reminder of your goals will help you stay focused on achieving them. Most successful people wouldn't be without their to-do list in some form. You shouldn't either.

Once you have a working to-do list, no matter how long or how many days it will take to accomplish it, you can add other daily habits that support completion of your tasks. What are some strategies that successful people use?

- Answer your email after 12 noon, once you've accomplished the important tasks of the day.
- Do the most difficult task first thing in the morning.
- Get comfortable with having difficult conversations so you won't put them off.
- Schedule appointments later in the week after you've accomplished your most important tasks.

I am giving my full attention to this current moment in my life.

Whatever you experience during the last 45 minutes of your day has the greatest effect on your sleep. If it's the evening news, that's what will be etched onto your subconscious—war, crime, natural disasters, and government scandals. Instead, why not take that time to put thoughts into your subconscious that will help propel you forward toward your goals? A powerful exercise called the Evening Review will help you initiate new, positive behaviors.

Sit with your eyes closed, breathe deeply, and give yourself one of the following directives:

- Show me where I could have been more effective today.
- Show me where I could have been more loving today.
- Show me where I could have been more assertive today.
- Show me where I could have been more patient or helpful today.

As events come to mind, observe them but don't be judgmental or critical. Replay them the way you wish you would have done them if you had been more aware or intentional.

> *As I sit and quietly contemplate my day,*
> *I am bringing more focus and awareness to*
> *my mind with every breath I take.*

Week 28

Clean Up Your Messes and Your Incompletes

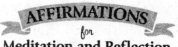

AFFIRMATIONS
for
Meditation and Reflection

I am finding ways to clean up my messes and incompletes so that I have more time to focus on my goals.

I am joyfully attracting more abundance and new relationships into my life as I complete, dump, or delegate paperwork and clutter.

I am continually clearing out old things in my life to make space for the new things that I want.

> *Cluttered closets mean a*
> *cluttered mind.*
>
> —LOUISE HAY
> American motivational author and
> founder of Hay House Publishing

*Y*our memory bank is made up of what I call "attention units." You can only pay attention to a limited number of things at once, and every item on your to-do list—whether work-related or home projects or personal and family issues—takes up a certain number of attention units. Incompletes and messes like unfinished paperwork, contracts that need completing, clutter, unresolved relationship issues, and ongoing home renovations consume precious attention units that you need in order to achieve your goals. We can't embrace our exciting future if there are things left unfinished that nag us, annoy us, and take our focus away.

So why do we accept incompletions and messy environments? Sometimes the reason is emotional or psychological. We might be indecisive on how to proceed. Sometimes we just plain procrastinate. But 20 things completed is better than 50 things half-completed, so with this week's affirmations, we're going to work on developing your "completion consciousness."

> **I am finding ways to clean up my**
> **messes and incompletes so that I have**
> **more time to focus on my goals.**

There's a simple rule about completion that will help you finish what you start, it's called "The Four D's of Completion." They are: Do It, Delegate It, Delay It, or Dump It.

As soon as you pick up a piece of paper, make a decision about it. If you can handle it quickly, do it right away. If it's something someone else can do for you, delegate it right away. You may have to delay it if it requires scheduling and planning. Or, if it's something you probably will never actually get around to doing, regardless of your good intentions, dump it right away. The goal is to get it off your desk as soon as you can.

The same goes for your home. Worn-out clothes, old toys, paperwork, overstuffed bookshelves and cluttered coffee tables, counter tops, and garages also use up valuable attention units. And if you're one of those people who support the mini-storage industry, more than likely your storage unit is filled with things you don't really need and can barely remember you own.

If you want new things to come into your life, you're going to have to make room for them. Evaluate and confront the psychological or physical reasons you haven't let these old, unwanted things go. Incompletes like clutter keep abundance at a distance —address them, let go of them, and make room for your present and fabulous future.

> *I am joyfully attracting more abundance and new relationships into my life as I complete, dump, or delegate paperwork and clutter.*

How much do you need to do, delegate, delay, or dump in order to complete the past and make room for new activity and excitement in your life? Make a list—use the checklist below to inspire your thinking—then write down how you plan to accomplish each one. Do the ones that will immediately free up the most mental or physical space first.

- Business activities that need completion
- Unpaid debts or financial commitments
- Closets stuffed with clothes that don't fit
- Disorganized tax records
- "Junk drawers" full of useless items
- Desk that's cluttered or disorganized
- Family pictures that need an album

One more thing—you know those little things around the house that are daily irritants? A screen door that needs repair, a tub that needs recaulking . . . make a plan to fix them. You could hire a handyman or professional organizer to help you fix things or declutter. If you can't afford it, ask a friend, neighbor, or a family member to help, and free up some space for more important things—like your future!

> *I am continually clearing out old things in my life to make space for the new things that I want.*

Week 29

Complete the Past So You Can Embrace the Future

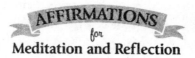

AFFIRMATIONS
for
Meditation and Reflection

I am releasing the past and becoming lighter and happier as I embrace my exciting future.

I am forgiving and letting go of past hurts, and re-directing my energy toward positive, goal-oriented activities.

I am creating the future I really want, free of past hurts, with my full attention on the present.

> *None of us can change our yesterdays but*
> *all of us can change our tomorrows.*
>
> —GENERAL COLIN POWELL
> Former Secretary of State

When someone has hurt you deeply—or even harmed you physically or emotionally—it's hard to let go of the past and move forward to living a successful life. The Total Truth Process is a tool that will enable you to release any negative emotions from your past. By expressing all of your true feelings to the person who hurt you, you can move past the hurt and reclaim the naturally optimistic person you are meant to be.

When you speak to the person (you can also write a Total Truth Letter to send them, share with them, or for yourself alone), be sure to address the negative emotions you're carrying by completing these phrases:

- **Anger and resentment:** *I'm angry that* or *I resent that . . .*
- **Hurt:** *I feel sad when . . .* or *It hurts me when . . .*
- **Fear:** *I was afraid that . . .* or *I feel scared when . . .*
- **Regret and remorse:** *I'm sorry that . . .*
- **Wants:** *All I ever wanted . . .* or *I deserve . . .*
- **Love, compassion, forgiveness:** *I forgive you for . . .*

I am releasing the past and becoming lighter and happier as I embrace my exciting future.

W e've talked before about the importance of positive energy and the reciprocal energy that flows back to you when you stay upbeat. But being unforgiving, angry, or negative about a past hurt follows the same Law of Attraction—you'll only attract more of the same into your life.

Award-winning author Isabelle Holland said, "As long as you don't forgive, who and whatever it is will occupy rent-free space in your head." When you do forgive, it allows you to live in the present where you can take action and create a successful future for yourself, your family, and your company. Here's how:

1) Acknowledge your anger and resentment.

2) Acknowledge the hurt and pain it created.

3) Acknowledge the fears and self-doubts it created.

4) Acknowledge any part you may have had in letting the behavior or event occur or continue.

5) Acknowledge what you wanted and didn't get, then attempt to understand where the other person was coming from at the time and the needs he was trying to meet by his behavior.

6) Let go and forgive the person.

> *I am forgiving and letting go of past hurts, and re-directing my energy toward positive, goal-oriented activities.*

Over the years, I have sought—and found—thousands upon thousands of inspirational stories for the *Chicken Soup for the Soul* books, and I learned that human beings have the potential to forgive anything or anyone, no matter how brutal or tragic.

About 10 years ago, I learned a technique called *tapping therapy* that proved to be a breakthrough for many people for whom getting beyond their "past" was exceptionally difficult and painful. "Tapping" is a drug-free and non-invasive way to reduce or eliminate post-traumatic stress. The technique is so powerful that it has been used with genocide victims in Rwanda and Bosnia, by a trainer of the British Special Forces in the Congo, and with returning U.S. soldiers with PTSD. Tapping stimulates the body's own ability to release stored pain of any kind—including emotional pain which the body also stores. The results are absolutely miraculous!

In my book *Tapping into Ultimate Success** you can learn how to use tapping to free yourself from stress, emotional hurts and anxieties and, ultimately, help you succeed.

> *I am creating the future I really want, free of past hurts, with my full attention on the present.*

---

* *Tapping into Ultimate Success: How to Overcome Any Obstacle and Skyrocket Your Results* by Jack Canfield with Pamela Bruner (Hay House, 2012).

Week 30

If It's Not Working, Face It

AFFIRMATIONS
for
Meditation and Reflection

I am acknowledging when something isn't working for me, and taking action to fix it, no matter how uncomfortable or challenging it might be.

I am recognizing situations that I am afraid to deal with, boldly facing my fears and dealing with them anyway.

When something goes wrong, I am committed to finding out the reason why and taking prompt steps to fix it.

*Our lives improve only when we take chances—
and the first and most difficult risk we can
take is to be honest with ourselves.*

—WALTER ANDERSON
Author of *The Confidence Course,* former editor of
Parade magazine and a lifelong literacy advocate

When things aren't going your way, it's often difficult to face them—particularly if you've developed your other success skills and are accustomed to believing it's possible, going the extra mile, and being persistent. But sometimes, things are just a train wreck. Sometimes, there's just no fixing them—other than to wrap up your involvement, get them to a stable point, and move on. At other times, facing what's not working actually brings about new solutions or even better outcomes than you were working toward. But you have to recognize these situations in the first place. And that can be very difficult.

Back in *Week 1: Take 100% Responsibility for Your Future,* we talked about internal and external alerts—those gut feelings you have or the suspicious charges on your household checking account. These patterns and signals hint that something isn't right.

Don't ignore these alerts—things will only get worse. If you are committed to living a truly successful life, you'll face facts and be totally honest with yourself.

I am acknowledging when something isn't working for me, and taking action to fix it, no matter how uncomfortable or challenging it might be.

dmitting that something isn't working usually requires that you also *do something about it*, and often that "something" is uncomfortable: exercising more self-discipline, verbally confronting someone, quitting your job, or grounding your teenager. Often, because facing these situations is so unpleasant, sometimes we defend tolerating them instead of admitting that they don't work.

How does denial actually represent itself? Through myths that we hide behind and platitudes that sound reasonable. Phrases such as these are telltale signs:

- "She's 18. We can't control her forever."
- "I'm not complaining, I'm just venting."
- "Can you ask Jonathan? That's not under my department."
- "Boys will be boys."
- "Someone smarter than me is supposed to prevent that."
- "She's just drowning her sorrows."
- "Mom's neighbors check on her."
- "I know, but he's pretty stressed out at work right now."

The truth is, if we could get past the denial and just face the facts, the situation would be less painful to resolve, our integrity would increase, and we'd feel better about ourselves. But first we have to get past denial.

> *I am recognizing situations that I am afraid to deal with, boldly facing my fears and dealing with them anyway.*

 liminating denial requires that you learn to recognize bad situations and react right away. It's always surprising how many people find recognition and decision difficult. You don't want to admit that your marriage is failing because you'd have to face the emotional stress of a divorce—especially if you have children. But, once you face facts, the ultimate solution might actually be marriage counseling or a commitment to setting new goals and boundaries together. Isn't it better to know instead of living in fear?

The more you commit to facing uncomfortable situations, the better you will get at it. And the sooner you react, the easier it is to clean up these situations. Take time now to make a list of what isn't working in your life—focusing specifically on the seven major areas where you set goals: financial, career or business, fun and recreation, health, relationships, personal growth, and making a difference. Choose one item at a time, decide what needs to be done to fix it, then make a plan and do it. Work down your list until you get them all resolved—you will feel an amazing sense of freedom as you do.

> *When something goes wrong,*
> *I am committed to finding out the reason*
> *why and taking prompt steps to fix it.*

Week 31

Transform Your Inner Critic into an Inner Coach

AFFIRMATIONS
for
Meditation and Reflection

I am only allowing thoughts that serve me in creating greater success and happiness in my life.

I am joyfully looking for the good in myself and others, which makes me feel more appreciative and optimistic.

I am training my inner critic to act as a supportive inner coach by filling my thoughts and self-talk with encouragement and confidence.

A man is literally what he thinks.

—JAMES ALLEN
Author of *As a Man Thinketh*

Research indicates that you talk to yourself about 50,000 times a day. That's a lot of chatter going on in your head! But that research also indicates that about 80% of these internal lectures are negative: *I'm always late . . . Oh great, another bad hair day . . . I shouldn't have said that . . . I'll never lose this weight.* Learning to quiet your inner critic and replace that negative internal dialog with positive self-talk will help you stay in a better, more successful frame of mind.

After all, we know that our thoughts have a powerful effect on our attitude, motivation, physiology, and even our biochemistry. Since our thoughts actually control our behavior, negative thoughts can make us anxious, scared, sweat, spill things, forget our lines, and more. Consider polygraph tests—your body reacts to your thoughts, which are responding to the questions being asked. Your hands get colder, your blood pressure rises, and other physiological responses occur. Similarly, your body responds to *positive* stimuli, too—you feel relaxed, centered, and cheerful. Reinforce that response experience through positive self-talk— you have thousands of opportunities every day to practice until it becomes a habit!

I am only allowing thoughts that serve me in creating greater success and happiness in my life.

You are in charge of your own thoughts and self-talk, and you can choose what to believe. Be aware of these types of negative thinking so you can avoid them:

- **Always-or-Never.** If you think that something will always happen or you'll never get what you want, that's self-sabotage. Stop using words like *always, never* and *every time*.

- **Focusing on the Negative.** Choose to focus on the positive. You'll become more appreciative and optimistic, which will attract more good to you.

- **Catastrophic Predicting.** Do you create the worst possible scenario in your mind, which you accept as a certainty?

- **Mind Reading.** Unless you're a psychic, you can't read anyone else's mind. You don't know what another person is thinking unless he or she tells you. Don't do it.

- **Guilt-Tripping.** Words such as *should, must, ought to,* and *have to* will lead to guilt, which is never productive. Guilt is an emotional barrier to success.

- **Labeling.** By labeling yourself or someone else with a derogatory term like *jerk, idiot,* or *arrogant,* you can't see the uniqueness of the person or situation.

- **Personalizing.** Things happen every day that aren't directed at you personally, so don't assign a personal meaning to a neutral event. There are hundreds of explanations for other people's actions other than what your negative thoughts conjure up.

> *I am joyfully looking for the good in myself and others, which makes me feel more appreciative and optimistic.*

What if you could transform your inner critic into an inner coach who supports and encourages you and gives you confidence? With a little awareness, attention, and focus, you can do it.

Even though it chastises and judges you, your inner critic actually has your best interests in mind—it wants you to benefit from better behavior—only you have to train it to start telling you the *whole* truth. Let's say you need to lose 20 pounds and you haven't been to the gym in several months. Your inner critic may be angry at you for not taking better care of yourself, and it may even call you a lazy slob for not having enough self-discipline. But its underlying emotion is actually, *I love you and I want you to be healthy so you are around for a long time; I want you to look good, have lots of energy, and be happy.*

Sounds like a completely different message, doesn't it?

Redirecting the judgmental voice of your inner critic to the supportive, corrective voice of your inner coach takes awareness and persistence. Once you start the process and have some experience making the transition, the conversation will switch to a non-emotional discussion of opportunities for improvement, instead of criticism. It's like having a life coach in your head—for free!

> *I am training my inner critic to act as a supportive inner coach by filling my thoughts and self-talk with encouragement and confidence.*

Week
32

Develop New Success Habits

I am developing new habits of focused action and personal discipline and maintaining high levels of energy that contribute significantly to my success.

I am consciously eliminating habits that inhibit my growth and limit my success.

I am systematically adding one new beneficial habit at a time that will dramatically improve my life.

*The individual who wants to reach the top
in business must appreciate the might and force of habit.
He must be quick to break those habits that can
break him—and hasten to adopt those practices
that will become the habits that help him
achieve the success he desires.*

—J. PAUL GETTY
Founder of Getty Oil Company and philanthropist

One of the problems of people with bad habits is that the results of their poor habits often aren't conspicuous until much later in life. But when you have chronic bad habits, like it or not, life will eventually deliver the consequences. Negative habits breed negative consequences; positive habits breed positive consequences.

Successful people don't just drift to the top—they apply focused attention, self-discipline, and energy to get there. Since habits determine our outcomes, successful people have to be hyper-aware of their habits and behaviors.

Start your habit-driven path to success by adding one new habit every quarter; research shows that if you repeat a new behavior for 13 weeks, it will be yours for life. Today is the day to start.

*I am developing new habits of focused
action and personal discipline and maintaining
high levels of energy that contribute
significantly to my success.*

Robert J. Ringer, author of *Million Dollar Habits*, said, "Success is a matter of understanding and religiously practicing specific, simple habits that always lead to success." According to psychologists, up to 90% of our behavior is habitual. Think about that—from waking up in the morning, to eating breakfast, to driving to work, to going shopping, to cooking or eating out, to how you spend your weekends, to all the little rituals you have before going to sleep. Habits are what keep you going—they allow you to do more than one thing at a time and they keep your life in order. But, some habits don't benefit you at all and you may not even be aware of them—if they're detrimental to your success, it's time to take an inventory and replace them with better habits that move you forward.

We all have good habits and bad habits—but every single one of them is responsible for where and who you are today. Every habit produces some form of result. Because of that, it's imperative that you become more aware of your habits—especially the negative ones that can hold you back from success.

> *I am consciously eliminating habits*
> *that inhibit my growth and limit my success.*

There are two steps to implementing new, beneficial habits that will take you in a forward direction. Step One is to make a list of all your *bad habits* that contribute nothing beneficial to your life—and that negatively impact your current situation and your future. Be objective about your limiting habits—review the list below for common pitfalls:

- Procrastinating or putting off difficult conversations
- Taking calls during meetings or dinner
- Working during vacations
- Spending beyond your budget
- Reading email first thing in the morning
- Arriving late for conference calls
- Eating junk food more than once a week
- Filing taxes or paying bills at the last minute

Once you've made your list and identified negative habits, the second step is to choose more productive success habits and develop systems to support them. If you used this strategy to implement just four new success habits a year—one every quarter—in five years you would have 20 new habits that could bring you wealth, health, happiness, and a host of new opportunities.

> *I am systematically adding one*
> *new beneficial habit at a time that will*
> *dramatically improve my life.*

Week 33

99% Is a Bitch, 100% Is a Breeze

I am enthusiastically giving 100% to carrying out my commitments every day.

I am practicing the "no exceptions" rule in order to keep my commitments and achieve all my goals.

I am committed to excellence in everything I do, which is positively impacting every aspect of my life, my career, my results, and my reputation.

*If you make the unconditional commitment
to reach your most important goals, if the strength
of your decision is sufficient, you will find the
way and the power to achieve your goals.*

—ROBERT CONKLIN
Creator of the Adventures in Attitudes
program used in companies worldwide

*E*very day people wake up and fight with themselves over whether or not they will keep their commitments and action plans. The victory always goes to the ones who have a "no matter what" attitude and take their 100% commitment seriously.

I admit that starting out can be a bit shaky sometimes—you might need an extra push at first—but once you get moving, it gets much easier. Depending on what you have committed to, instead of daily (like going to the gym, for instance), you may opt for five times a week or every other day (like having a salad for lunch).

Some commitments require daily practice. Working on your to-do-list is one of them, meditation or prayer is another, repeating your affirmations throughout the day is a given. Today, decide to give 100% to your commitments.

*I am enthusiastically giving 100% to carrying
out my commitments every day.*

There are some commitments that are entirely useless *unless* you give them 100%. Think about giving less than your all when it comes to quitting smoking, or texting while skiing, or meditating, or motorcycle racing. It just can't work, it would be impossible to succeed.

More often than we realize, we throw obstacles into our own paths that trip us up, delay our growth, and make things more difficult—impossible even. You drive to work with smokers, you can't walk away from your phone for 10 minutes, you allow the dog to distract you when you're meditating, or you don't maintain your engine or tires properly before you hit the speedway. They are all recipes for disaster.

And then there are roadblocks that we allow other people to place in front of us. A neighbor asks you to help set up a new printer right in the middle of your family time, or your teenager starts an argument just as you're heading to work, or a friend invites you over for lasagna just as you've started your new diet. You have to learn to say no (maybe another time?) because anything else strips your commitment and spells failure.

No one can achieve your goals and dreams for you, and no one can commit to their success, other than you. You are the one who determines your destiny.

> *I am practicing the "no exceptions" rule in order to keep my commitments and achieve all my goals.*

Successful people don't accept exceptions. Once they make a commitment to something, it's non-negotiable. If you make the 100% commitment to exercise every day, you will do it no matter what—even if you have an early morning appointment, or it's raining, or you just don't feel like doing it. When you're committed to meditate every day for 30 minutes, work on your to-do-list, make 10 new sales calls, practice the piano five days a week, or whatever it may be—only 100% commitment will do.

One final thing: Always honor your agreements and deliver on your word. Self-confidence, integrity, and motivation are the rewards for doing so, all of which have a wonderful impact on your reputation, and that's rewarding, too.

> *I am committed to excellence*
> *in everything I do, which is positively*
> *impacting every aspect of my life, my career,*
> *my results, and my reputation.*

Week 34

Learn More to Earn More

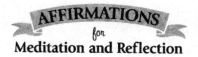

AFFIRMATIONS
for
Meditation and Reflection

I am happily committed to lifelong learning and self-improvement.

I am continually increasing my knowledge, which substantially increases my potential to succeed.

I am choosing to be teachable so that I can constantly learn and grow.

If I am through learning, I am through.

—JOHN WOODEN
Legendary UCLA basketball coach
who won 10 NCAA championships

any people resist the idea of continuous learning. They think it means going back to college or even starting college at mid-life. Although that's not necessarily a bad idea, that's not solely what "lifelong learning" means. Information is power, and those who have a wealth of information have a great advantage over those who don't. What are some excellent ways to acquire knowledge and get ahead of the game?

Make television time learning time: The average person watches six hours of TV a day—that's the *average*. My mentor W. Clement Stone once asked me to eliminate one hour of television a day to create an extra 365 hours per year to accomplish whatever is most important to me. That's over two months of additional time per year to focus on my goals. I'm asking you to do the same.

Now that we've found an extra two months to use for learning, we're going to discover ways to fill that time with educational and informational benefits that move you faster toward your goals.

> **I am happily committed to lifelong learning and self-improvement.**

*T*oday you'll put into action the same learning methods that top achievers use.

- **Leaders are readers:** Dr. John Demartini, one of the wisest, brightest, and most successful people I know, once said, "You can't put your hand in a pot of glue without some of that glue sticking." If you used that one extra hour a day to stick your head in a book, before long you would be in the top 1% of experts in your field!

- **Study the lives of great people:** There is much to learn from biographies, no matter what the subject's skills or accomplishments are: sports, politics, spirituality, business —they are all fascinating.

- **A weekly system for getting smart:** At *www.TheSuccess Principles.com/resources* you will find an extensive reading list of timeless classics and other books that contain some of the latest breakthroughs in the psychology of achievement, neuroscience, nutrition, and more. Books can be an expensive investment, so make use of your local libraries if it helps—or buy e-books, which are less expensive.

> *I am continually increasing my knowledge, which substantially increases my potential to succeed.*

here are endless ways to increase your knowledge and build a lifelong learning program. Let's look at a few more options:

 Get out and mix in: Attend success rallies, conferences, and retreats. From national symposiums to local talks and lectures, there are enough events available that you could probably attend one every weekday—plus weekends!

Attend human potential trainings: These are personal development seminars that focus on improving your ability, mind-set, network, and motivation to succeed. Everyone needs outside influences to help them break old habits and create new ways of thinking and behaving.

Be teachable: To learn and grow in life you have to be teachable. Every situation presents an opportunity to learn and every person has something they can teach you. Sometimes we lack the humility to learn from or see the potential in others, but when we adopt that kind of attitude, we become arrogant and unteachable. You don't know everything —no one does. Be open to learning no matter with whom or where you are.

> *I am choosing to be teachable so that*
> *I can constantly learn and grow.*

Week 35

Maintain Your Passion and Enthusiasm

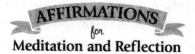

Meditation and Reflection

I am joyful knowing that I'm already a success when I follow my heart and do what I love.

I am enjoying my work so much that I am eager to get up every morning and get started.

I feel happy and fulfilled because I am doing what I was born to do.

Enthusiasm is one of the most powerful engines of success. When you do a thing, do it with all your might. Put your whole soul into it. Stamp it with your own personality. Be active, be energetic, be enthusiastic and faithful, and you will accomplish your object. Nothing great was ever achieved without enthusiasm.

—RALPH WALDO EMERSON
American essayist and poet

When you are happily doing what you love to do, you've already won. When you do something with passion and perseverance, you're already a success. True passion comes from within; it has a spiritual quality, and it can motivate you to accomplish incredible feats of success.

I'm sure you have met people who are passionate and enthusiastic about what they do. They have purpose and they are totally committed to their work. Caring about what you do, following your heart, and trusting your own ideas of what makes you happy will foster enthusiasm and passion in your life. It comes not just from enjoying your work but also in discovering what else you enjoy, and doing what you were born to do.

This week, we'll talk about passion and enthusiasm and how you can develop it, keep it alive, and even pass it on to others.

> *I am joyful knowing that I'm already a success when I follow my heart and do what I love.*

*D*eveloping passion for the most important areas of your life will make your dreams and goals not only more attainable but it will also make the journey a lot more entertaining, relaxed, and fulfilling.

Take a look at the key areas of your life: your work, your marriage, your friendships, leisure time, and other associations, whether they are professional, religious, or civic. Where do you lack passion and enthusiasm? What would you be doing differently that you think might bring you those qualities? What can you change, stop doing, or start doing that would make your life different? People who are passionate about what they are doing *are doing what they love!* They have found a way to make a living at it. If you love what you do but you're not feeling fulfilled, take a hard look at what has become a roadblock for you and deal with it.

When do you find that you are the happiest? What are you doing, feeling, thinking—and who are you with? Those are indicators of what you are attracted to and what could potentially bring more abundance and joy into your life—and the lives of those around you. Is there a way to integrate any of those elements into other areas of your life?

If you spend the time to really evaluate some of these issues and emotions, you will start to see pathways that will lead you to where you truly want to be.

I am enjoying my work so much that I am eager to get up every morning and get started.

So, how do you maintain joy and passion in your life every day? We talked about a few of the answers in earlier chapters: discovering your true purpose, deciding what you really want, believing anything is possible, and believing in yourself, to name a few.

Another way to succeed is to reconnect with your original purpose for doing whatever it is you are doing. Before it got to be a run-of-the-mill task or just a boring necessity, there was a reason that you did it—there was a deeper purpose that turned those have-to-dos into want-to-dos. What was it?

Most of the time, lack of passion and enthusiasm stem from your attitude. You have total control over your attitude—you can be miserable and grumpy about a situation or you can choose to be positive and look for benefits and unexpected opportunities.

And here's a bonus to consider. When you live with joy, gratitude, and enthusiasm, it's impossible to keep it to yourself. You become a magnet for others who will be drawn to your energy—often in a way that benefits *you*.

> *I feel happy and fulfilled because I am*
> *doing what I was born to do.*

Week 36

Stay Focused on Your Core Genius

I am confidently delegating things that get in the way of me staying focused on my core genius.

I am enjoying more free time and I am more productive when I delegate minor tasks to others.

I am turning over complete responsibility on less productive tasks so I can work on the things that make me happy and that I'm good at.

Success follows doing what you want to do.
There is no other way to be successful.

—MALCOLM S. FORBES
Publisher of *Forbes* magazine

o you know what your core genius is? It's the one thing that you love to do and do so well, that you hardly feel like charging people for it. It's effortless and fun—and could be your life's work if you could find a way to make it your livelihood. Successful people recognize the value of their core genius and do everything they can to spend all of their time doing it—because that's where the financial rewards and the joy are.

A lot of people (probably most) go through life doing *everything*. They spend their time on menial things that they don't enjoy doing and that provide no financial reward (or any reward, for that matter). Their time is consumed with tasks they're bad at and that could be done better, faster, and more economically by someone else. Their core genius gets pushed to the margins while they spend hours doing less important and fulfilling tasks.

When you concentrate on doing what you love to do, not only will you be more productive, you will find that life is much more enjoyable, too.

I am confidently delegating things
that get in the way of me staying
focused on my core genius.

*L*et's get to the root of why most people haven't arranged their lives to focus 100% on their core genius. Why don't people delegate tasks?

- **They're afraid to give up control, even of tasks they hate doing:** While someone else won't do it exactly like you would, there are many ways to accomplish something. Different isn't *wrong*, it could even be *better*.

- **They're reluctant to spend the money for help:** Investing your time where you produce the greatest results, like increased income, likely means spending a smaller amount of money with people who can free up your time.

- **They don't want to let go.** Many people are control freaks and hoarders of *everything*. Let the little things go; they don't contribute to your overall success and happiness.

- **They've made a habit of doing it:** You want to create good habits to replace your poor habits, remember? Doing something out of routine is unproductive and can become a pretty significant obstacle to reaching your goals. Those are destructive habits and it's time to quit.

I am enjoying more free time and I am more productive when I delegate minor tasks to others.

*L*et's say you've written your first book and you're now eager to begin adding other activities to your authoring career: speaking engagements, writing a newspaper column, doing coaching, and developing a training program for corporations. You need to cold-call event planners, find coaching clients, write and film training modules for corporations, and so on—but on top of all that, you're still running a small business *and* have a husband and two small children who need your attention. So, instead of spending your time booking speeches and writing corporate materials, you're lucky to get anything done. But you *could* be closing two or three speeches a week if you focused your time and attention on what you're best at and what you love to do the most. Looking at the big picture, wouldn't it be worth hiring a part-time mother's helper or additional person at your business—or doing whatever it takes—so you can focus on your new career?

Take a look at your life—both professional and personal—and identify these three things: (1) What you enjoy doing most, (2) What you enjoy doing least, and (3) How you can move those less meaningful and unproductive tasks off your plate and delegate them to someone else. The goal is to do more of #1: What you enjoy doing most.

> *I am turning over complete responsibility on less productive tasks so I can work on the things that make me happy and that I'm good at.*

Week 37

Reassess Your Time Commitments

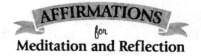

AFFIRMATIONS
for
Meditation and Reflection

I am creating superior results by maintaining balance between time spent at work, time with my family, and time just for me.

I highly value my Free Days and Focus Days, using my Buffer Days to plan, prepare, build new skills, and delegate nonessential tasks to others.

I am joyfully structuring my time to get the most out of my Focus Days with abundant time to pursue my personal interests.

> *The world is entering a new time-zone and*
> *one of the most difficult adjustments people must*
> *make is in their fundamental concepts and*
> *beliefs about the management of time.*
>
> —DAN SULLIVAN
> Founder and president, The Strategic Coach

This Principle, which is based on the work of Dan Sullivan, president of The Strategic Coach, will help you approach time management and scheduling differently. First, let's look into "vacation time."

According to a study by the U.S. Travel Association's Project Time Off, 54% of employees ended 2016 with unused time off. Not good—and here's why: If you don't take your time off, you are more likely to get burned out, get sick, and have your relationships suffer. The problem is not just unused vacation days; people are also reluctant to take any days for themselves—even if it's on their scheduled day off. Everyone needs a complete Free Day now and then—free of business-related meetings, reading, phone calls, and emails—because those days allow you to return to work refreshed, more creative, and more enthusiastic. And that benefits you, your family, your colleagues, your clients, and everyone else you interact with.

> *I am creating superior results by maintaining*
> *balance between time spent at work, time*
> *with my family, and time just for me.*

*I*f you really want to make the most of your time and talents, you need to look at how you use them. My second recommendation is to schedule Buffer Days.* In a five-day workweek, you need to schedule a day or two for doing things that prepare you for your Focus Days—days where you focus on using your core genius to produce bottom-line results.

Buffer Days are set aside for doing things like traveling, training, scheduling, attending meetings—any task or activity that will free your time and help you make your Focus Days as productive as possible. For me, a Buffer Day might include outlining a new speech, taking a seminar to improve my training skills, planning how to maximize sales of our books and audio programs at my next training, conducting research, or any number of projects that support me in working on my core genius during my Focus Days.

What are some of the projects that would fall into your Buffer Days? The key is to do things that will free up your Free Days and your Focus Days so you can use them for what they were intended—producing your most important bottom-line results.

> *I highly value my Free Days and Focus Days, using my Buffer Days to plan, prepare, build new skills, and delegate nonessential tasks to others.*

---

* Free Days, Focus Days, and Buffer Days are registered trademarks of The Strategic Coach, Inc. All rights reserved. I am grateful to Dan Sullivan for his Entrepreneurial Time System that teaches these concepts. For more information on The Strategic Coach Program, go to *www.thestrategiccoach.com*.

ow, let's take a look at Focus Days—where you focus at least 80% of your time on your core genius. These should be incredibly exciting days, ones you look to with anticipation and passion. These are your money days when you get to practice the skill that you are best at—the one you love, the one you were born to do.

The key to getting more Focus Days and Free Days is to schedule them . . . in ink. First, let's do a short but helpful exercise for clarification: 1) List the three best Focus Days you've ever had. 2) Write down the common elements. 3) Plan more perfect Focus Days—you now have excellent insight as to what made them so great. (You should do this with your Free Days also.)

The key to all of this is to be more intentional in the way you structure your time. Start today and take control of your time and your life so you maximize your results and income—make every minute of your days count. Only you have the information you need to succeed—your goals and dreams, your natural talent, your self-confidence, and your belief that you can accomplish anything that you set your mind to do.

One final suggestion: Begin by scheduling four vacations over the next year—from a few long weekends to your dream vacation. It won't happen unless you sit down and make a plan!

> *I am joyfully structuring my time to get the most out of my Focus Days with abundant time to pursue my personal interests.*

Week 38

Say "No" to Distractions

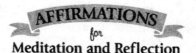

AFFIRMATIONS
for
Meditation and Reflection

I am consciously eliminating from my life those things that steal my time—I am saying no without excuses and apologies and it feels great!

I am learning to graciously say no to people and set policies about what I don't do so that others understand and support my boundaries.

I am confidently saying no without guilt to things that consume my time and energy so that I'm ready to take advantage of the great things waiting for me to accept them.

> *You don't have to let yourself be terrorized by*
> *other people's expectations of you.*
>
> —SUE PATTON THOELE
> Author of *The Courage to Be Yourself*

We live in a highly competitive and overstimulated world—you can be reached 24/7 by cell phone, text, email, and social media—at a client's office, in your car, on the golf course, in the restroom (and even in church or the movies if you forget to turn your ringer off). What's more, call-waiting beeps during important conversations, breaking your chain of thought in an instant.

With all the distractions and encroachments on our time, why is it so hard to say no? We let less important things break into our schedules and infringe upon our day, then instantly regret it.

Why can't we just say no?

Saying no without ambiguity is one of the hallmarks of successful people who are in control of their day and their future. It's not easy—in fact, we seem to be wired to accept every request even though it comes at great cost to ourselves and our families. Today, let's focus on the affirmation below and prepare for change.

> *I am consciously eliminating from*
> *my life those things that steal my time—*
> *I am saying no without excuses and*
> *apologies and it feels great!*

o you sometimes feel that everyone wants a piece of you? Your boss needs last-minute help with a presentation, your kids want a ride to a friend's for dinner, your parents need help at their house or with some paperwork, your sister wants to talk about her husband, and your coworkers want your help with a project that isn't even part of your job duties. On top of that, local charities want donations and your pets want to be walked, groomed, and petted nonstop.

To be successful, you are going to have to get good at saying no to all the people and "opportunities" that could devour you. And you've got to say no without feeling guilty. "No" is not only a complete sentence, it's an acceptable response. In fact, everyone should have a mental list of automatic declines—things they won't do under any circumstances. Do you?

> *I am learning to graciously say no to people and set policies about what I don't do so that others understand and support my boundaries.*

*H*ere are some tips for saying no without feeling guilty or fabricating an excuse:

- **"It's not against you, it's for me"**: Often we get so busy showing up for other people that there's no "me time" left in our week. But when you reply to requests with, "It's not against you, it's for me," you command respect for standing up for your own principles.

- **Say no to the good so you can say yes to the great**: It's easy to get caught up in situations and opportunities that are merely good while great opportunities eventually disappear simply because there's no time in your schedule.

- **Stop majoring in the minors**: Imagine how quickly you could reach your goals if you quit wasting time on minor tasks and instead focused solely on things that improve your life in the long run.

Establish new policies for saying no and develop the confidence to communicate this to your boss, coworkers, family, and friends, so you don't use all your available time for other people's dreams, goals, and priorities.

> *I am confidently saying no without guilt to things that consume my time and energy so that I'm ready to take advantage of the great things waiting for me to accept them.*

Week 39

Be a Leader Worthy of Followers

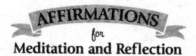

AFFIRMATIONS *for* **Meditation and Reflection**

I am communicating my vision clearly and passionately to others and they are trusting my leadership.

I feel courageous and inspired as I apply the principles of being a great leader.

I am experiencing my confidence continually growing as I coach others to success.

*The most dangerous leadership myth is
that leaders are born—that there is a genetic factor
to leadership. That's nonsense; in fact, the opposite
is true. Leaders are made rather than born.*

—WARREN BENNIS
Founding chairman at the Leadership Institute at
the University of Southern California

Success usually requires the help of others; therefore, most successful people are exceptional leaders who can effectively motivate others. They also have common traits:

- They have a clear and well-defined vision of the goals and future they're pursuing and they communicate that vision to others in ways that are compelling and exciting.
- They are masters at motivating people to join their team and commit 100%.
- They are excellent coaches; they can quickly spot potential in others and spur them to go the extra mile.
- They acknowledge the positive contribution of others.
- They hold the people they lead accountable, but more important, they hold themselves accountable.
- They inspire their people to grow as leaders, too.

> *I am communicating my vision clearly
> and passionately to others and they
> are trusting my leadership.*

K nowing how to be a successful leader will benefit you no matter where life takes you. Few of us are destined to become leaders on the level of Nelson Mandela or Mother Teresa, but we can all learn leadership skills that have a positive impact in our sphere of influence. How?

1) **Know your own strengths and weaknesses:** Great leaders understand themselves as well as others. They're realistic about their own skills and capabilities, and they keep their emotions in check during periods of intense pressure or rapid change, which creates a sense of safety for others. Admit that you don't know everything, be willing to be wrong, and always listen to feedback.

2) **Hold yourself accountable as well as others:** Take 100% responsibility for your actions and results. That's how you begin to build trust—by being reliable, punctual, and keeping your agreements. You also have to be courageous enough to hold others accountable for their actions and results.

3) **Inspire others with your clear and compelling vision:** Your followers must be able to see a successful future for themselves; they want to be smarter, better, stronger, more confident, and more competent.

I feel courageous and inspired as I apply the principles of being a great leader.

*H*ow else can you recognize a leader worth following? Here are three more qualities you should work hard to establish in your heart and mind:

1) **Listen for possibility:** People want to feel that you *hear* them—that their insights and opinions matter. Great leaders listen, not only to their team's ideas and concepts, but they also shift their own focus from listening for negative comments to listening for what is possible.

2) **Coach others for a leadership role:** You can't do everything yourself. But you *can coach others* to develop their own solutions and problem-solving abilities. When you develop other people as leaders, you free up your own time and focus for accomplishing *your* vision.

3) **Maintain an attitude of gratitude:** The easiest way to build trust, enthusiasm, and commitment is by practicing gratitude and acknowledging others. Experiencing and showing gratitude and appreciation improves your mood, makes you feel lighter, and helps you feel less stress.

Becoming a leader worth following will transform your future by attracting other optimistic people into your world who can help you achieve your goals faster.

> *I am experiencing my confidence continually growing as I coach others to success.*

Week 40

Create a Network of Mentors, Contacts, and Coaches

I am thrilled to be learning and growing under the wings of mentors who guide me toward success.

I look forward to networking and building strong relationships—that's how some of the most exciting and unexpected things happen.

With the expert guidance of my coach, I am joyfully leaping forward in every area of my life.

> *Study anyone who's great, and you'll find*
> *that they apprenticed to a master or several masters.*
> *Therefore, if you want to achieve greatness,*
> *renown, and superlative success, you*
> *must apprentice to a master.*
>
> —ROBERT ALLEN
> Coauthor of *The One Minute Millionaire*

Most people seek advice from their friends, spouse, or coworkers on issues they are facing. But unless you want recommendations on a movie, that's probably not the best group of people to ask for advice.

We have discussed how success leaves clues often in the form of people who have wisdom and experience they can share with you. Isn't it smarter to seek out one of these people who've already been down the road you're traveling? Make a list of the people you'd like to have mentor you—then ask them.

Many people have reached the pinnacle of their careers and are happy to impart what they've learned as a way to "give back" to their industry and the world. Make a commitment to identify three people you could ask to mentor you, then contact them with a specific request of an hour a month or an hour a quarter or a 15-minute call every few weeks.

> *I am thrilled to be learning and growing*
> *under the wings of mentors who*
> *guide me toward success.*

A dam Small, founder of Nashville Emerging Leaders said, "Networking is the single most powerful tactic to accelerate and sustain success for any individual or organization!" Business and careers are built on relationships; networking provides a platform to cultivate relationships. Plus, it also helps with:

- **Generating referrals and increased business:** Networking gives you high-quality referrals that are often prequalified.

- **Expanding opportunities:** Networking with other people in your industry—or fellow business owners—provides opportunities for joint ventures, partnerships, sales leads, and more.

- **Creating connections:** Remember the old adage "it's not *what* you know, it's *who* you know"? Well, it's true, but it's also *how well* you know someone that counts.

- **Obtaining useful advice:** Networking gives you unique opportunities to benefit from advice and expertise on business issues and even personal matters.

Use today's affirmation to focus on expanding your professional and personal network.

I look forward to networking and building strong relationships—that's how some of the most exciting and unexpected things happen.

Would you expect an athlete to make it to the Olympic Games without a coach? Or an NFL team to show up for a game without an entire cadre of coaches?

Well, coaching isn't just for sports. Business and personal coaches have been the "secret weapon" behind countless thousands of successful people—and hundreds of the world's top companies.

A good coach will help you clarify your vision, stay in your core genius, confront bad habits and destructive patterns of behavior, help you overcome roadblocks, push you to do your best, and show you how to work less and earn more.

I have experienced great success through being coached, and I have also been fantastically successful in coaching others. You can access information and read success stories online for the Canfield Coaching* program, which I developed to help people more easily implement success principles in their life.

> *With the expert guidance of my coach,*
> *I am joyfully leaping forward in*
> *every area of my life.*

---

* Visit the Canfield Coaching website at *www.canfieldcoaching.com*.

Week 41

Use the Power of the Master Mind

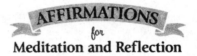

AFFIRMATIONS
for
Meditation and Reflection

I am experiencing the wonderful power that comes to us from each other and from above.

I believe that others who share my desire to be a positive influence will be attracted to me and exchange knowledge and resources.

I am joyfully connecting with my accountability partner who supports me and ensures that I achieve my goals and rise above setbacks.

*When two or more people . . . work toward a definite
objective or purpose, they place themselves in position,
through the alliance, to absorb power directly from
the great storehouse of Infinite Intelligence.*

—NAPOLEON HILL
Author of *Think and Grow Rich*

asterminding is a formidable tool and one of the most powerful strategies used throughout history by successful people. When high achievers are asked about the one thing that contributed the most to their becoming a millionaire, participation in a mastermind group is their primary answer.

The foundational philosophy of masterminding is that more can be achieved in less time when people work together—focusing energy, resources, knowledge, and insights on creating solutions and opportunities for one another—*even if they aren't in the same industry, life circumstances, or even the same town.* Napoleon Hill, author of the 1937 classic *Think and Grow Rich,* wrote that if, as a group, we are in tune with *the* Master Mind—that is, God, Source, Infinite Intelligence, Universal Power, or whatever term you use for the all-powerful creative life-force—we then have significantly more positive energy and power available to us, a power that can be focused on our success.

*I am experiencing the wonderful power that
comes to us from each other and from above.*

One of the best-known mastermind groups included Henry Ford, Thomas Edison, and Harvey Firestone, who met at their winter homes in Fort Meyers, Florida. Can you imagine the immense power in the room when *they* were together?

The ideal size of a mastermind group is five or six people who should meet together once a week, biweekly or at minimum, once per month. It's preferable to meet in person and experience the energy of being together, but it can also be done effectively through Skype, Face Time, or any one of many video communications programs. The group can (and should) consist of people from diverse backgrounds and industries in order to get the most out of the exchange of ideas, thoughts, solutions, contacts, and other resources. By forming or joining such a group, you'll benefit from the variety of unique perspectives and knowledge in the room, all of which can enhance your view of the world, advance your own goals, and create new opportunities more quickly and effectively.

Your ideal mastermind group should be made up of people who are already where you'd like to be in life or at least a level above you financially. Never talk yourself down when asking— self-confidence and positive energy will make you someone that others want to associate with.

> *I believe that others who share my desire to be a positive influence will be attracted to me and exchange knowledge and resources.*

*I*f you can't form a group right now, one alternative is to find an accountability partner—someone who's enthusiastic and supportive of your goals and with whom you can share progress or setbacks. Both of you agree to a plan that sets goals and targets that each of you are working toward achieving. You meet regularly in person or by telephone and hold one another accountable for making progress—meeting deadlines, accomplishing goals, and more.

Having an accountability partner encourages you to follow through on your plans—having to report to someone else provides a boost in motivation for getting things done. If you have a small business or work from home—let's say you have a two-person CPA agency, or you are a freelance writer who works solely from home, or a sales person who rarely goes to an "office"—having an accountability partner is an excellent idea. Knowing that you have to report on your productivity tomorrow makes you work harder and smarter today.

Here's another great reason for having an accountability partner: you have a sounding board—someone to listen to your new pitch, give you feedback on your new idea, share information, contacts, and resources.

I am joyfully connecting with my accountability partner who supports me and ensures that I achieve my goals and rise above setbacks.

Week
42

Listen to Your Gut Instincts

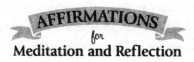

AFFIRMATIONS
for
Meditation and Reflection

I am committed to being super-successful—I have developed my intuition and learned to trust my instincts and follow my inner guidance.

As I meditate and become more spiritually attuned, I am connecting with my higher self through words, images, and sensations.

I have all the resources I need in my own mind; I am tapping into my intuition and achieving a greater level of success.

Brain researchers estimate that your unconscious database outweighs the conscious on an order exceeding ten million to one. This database is the source of your hidden, natural genius. In other words, a part of you is much smarter than you are. The wise people regularly consult that smarter part.

—MICHAEL J. GELB
Author of *How to Think Like Leonardo da Vinci*

*E*arly education and training taught us to look for answers outside ourselves, yet many of the most successful people in the world practice some type of daily meditation to access the vast resources and wisdom *inside* themselves. Most of them have actually learned to develop their intuition, follow their inner guidance, and trust their gut instincts. By using your intuition, you can make better decisions, be quicker at problem solving, access your creative genius, discern hidden motives in others, create winning strategies, visualize new opportunities, and make more money.

With today's affirmation, we'll begin focusing on connecting with your core self—looking inside instead of outside for answers to your questions.

I am committed to being super-successful— I have developed my intuition and learned to trust my instincts and follow my inner guidance.

*H*ave you ever been thinking about someone you haven't spoken to in a while and out of the blue, they call? Or maybe you've had an idea about how to move forward on a goal or project you're involved with—and the necessary resources magically show up? That was your intuition at work, and you can learn to tap into it at will to achieve greater success.

To connect with your natural intuition and untapped wisdom, allowing it to speak to you, you need to get quiet. So much of our day is a busy, harried, noise-filled existence. Meditation, on the other hand, removes distractions and deepens our intuition so we can better recognize subtle impulses, the sound of our higher self, or the voice of God speaking to us.

During your meditation time, ask it questions like:

- Should I take this job?

- Is there another way to approach this health condition?

- What should I do next?

When you get an answer, a feeling, or an idea out of the blue, write it down so you don't lose the information. Take immediate action on the ideas you get.

> *As I meditate and become more spiritually attuned, I am connecting with my higher self through words, images, and sensations.*

Trusting yourself is another form of trusting your intuition. The more trust you have, the more success you will have, too. You don't get credit for what stays in your mind, you get credit for what you write down and actually do.

Successful people not only inquire within and trust their intuition, they live in a state of mindfulness. Mind-set matters —a lot. Mindfulness is *a state of active, open, nonjudgmental attention on the present.* Even though you focus a lot of time on your future goals and how to achieve them, it is imperative that you stay grounded in the present—that you take action and maintain a growth-oriented mind-set.

Developing mindfulness, trusting your intuition, meditating, and learning to recognize answers, and inquiring within, will help you stay focused on doing the things that will get you where you want to go. In the meantime, remember that life is a dance, and mindfulness is taking the time to witness and enjoy that dance. Slowing down and being mindful in the present, will actually help you build a more successful future faster.

> *I have all the resources I need in my own mind; I am tapping into my intuition and achieving a greater level of success.*

Week 43

Listen to Learn

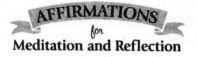

for
Meditation and Reflection

I am enjoying a deeper sense of fulfillment when actively listening to someone, who then feels fulfilled as a result of being truly heard.

I am practicing the art of arguing less and listening more.

I am learning to be caring and patient while actively listening to others express their feelings.

*The art of effective listening is essential to
clear communication, and clear communication is
necessary to management success.*

—JAMES CASH "J. C." PENNEY
Founded the J. C. Penney stores in 1902

*L*istening is something that goes beyond the hearing process—it requires concentration and attention for you to process meaning from words. According to Toastmasters International, there are four basic levels of hearing and listening:

1) **Non-listeners** are preoccupied with their own thoughts; they hear words but they don't listen to what is being said.

2) **Passive listeners** hear the words but don't fully absorb or understand them.

3) **Listeners** pay attention to the speaker but grasp only some of the message.

4) **Active listeners** are completely focused on the speaker and his body language. They understand the meaning of the words and the "message behind the words."

When you actively listen, you allow new ideas, opportunities, and solutions to filter into your awareness.

*I am enjoying a deeper sense of fulfillment
when actively listening to someone, who then
feels fulfilled as a result of being truly heard.*

Without mastering the art of active listening, not only will it take you longer to be successful, but you will impose limits on your ability to grow, learn, and earn the respect of others.

There are two requirements to being a good listener. The first one is *argue less and listen more*. Have you ever had to redo something because *that's not what was wanted?* Not delivering can be costly if payment is contingent on providing a product that your customer wants and will pay for. If you are a salaried employee, having to redo projects can be costly for the company and worse—it could cost you your job. Listen and repeat the request to verify that you're in agreement and you will eliminate or greatly reduce those situations.

The second requirement is to be *interested* rather than *interesting*. Some people seem to think that always presenting themselves in the best light, getting your story out first, self-promoting, and flaunting your expertise and intelligence with words and comments is the way to successful relationships with others. But the road to success is actually paved with humility—that is, focusing on others rather than on yourself.

> *I am practicing the art of arguing less and listening more.*

ere's a great technique that I learned from Dan Sullivan in his Strategic Coach Program* that will help you establish rapid rapport with another person. Ask them:

1) *If we were meeting three years from today, what has to have happened during that period for you to feel happy about your progress?*

2) *What are the biggest dangers you'll have to face and deal with in order to achieve that progress?*

3) *What are the biggest opportunities you'd have to focus on and capture to achieve those things?*

4) *What strengths will you need to reinforce and maximize and what skills and resources will you need to develop that you don't currently have in order to capture those opportunities?*

Asking those questions—and letting the other person talk without interruption—will enable him or her to go through a process of clarification and feel really heard by you.

> *I am learning to be caring*
> *and patient while actively listening*
> *to others express their feelings.*

---

* Learn more about Dan Sullivan and The Strategic Coach program by visiting *www.StrategicCoach.com.*

Have a Heart Talk

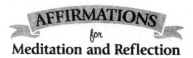

AFFIRMATIONS
for
Meditation and Reflection

I am creating a deeper level of connection and intimacy by freely expressing my true feelings.

As I participate in a Heart Talk, I am experiencing a deeper level of listening and a release of unexpressed emotions.

I am feeling free and optimistic as I willingly let go of any resentments and old issues during a Heart Talk.

*Most communication resembles a
Ping-Pong game in which people are merely
preparing to slam their next point across.*

—CLIFF DURFEE
Creator of the Heart Talk process

One of my favorite stories is about Nan-in, a Japanese master during the Meiji era, who one day welcomed a professor who came to inquire about Zen. Nan-in served tea. He poured his visitor's cup full, then kept on pouring. The professor watched the overflow until he could no longer restrain himself from saying, "It's overfull. No more will go in!"

"Like this cup," Nan-in said, "you are full. How can I show you Zen unless you first empty your cup?"

In far too many homes, businesses, schools, and other settings, there is no opportunity for people to express their feelings—their hopes, dreams, pains, and fears. As a result, they become filled beyond capacity until they are overflowing with their own priorities, problems, and worries.

People can't listen when they are bursting at the seams. They need an outlet to release their emotions before they can take in anything else. They need to open up and get what's bothering them off their chest in order to create space to listen and process what *you* have to say. You, and they, need a Heart Talk.

I am creating a deeper level of connection and intimacy by freely expressing my true feelings.

A Heart Talk is a process where eight agreements are strictly adhered to among 2 to 10 people—a larger group diminishes trust and can take a long time to complete. A Heart Talk supports constructive discussion of feelings and issues that limit creativity, teamwork and innovation. Heart Talks promote productivity and camaraderie and goodwill, which are vital to every organization and home.

A Heart Talk facilitates a deep level of communication without the fear of condemnation, interpretation, or being rushed. It's a powerful tool for bringing unexpressed emotions to the surface and developing rapport, understanding, and intimacy.

Heart Talks can be conducted for many purposes and are useful in finding solutions for a wide range of challenges, but they should be implemented before too much damage is done:

- At home after you recognize there is withheld hostility, fears, or distrust
- At the office, after an emotional event like layoffs, a merger, a natural disaster or other tragedy, the death of a coworker, even financial problems within the company
- When there is a conflict between two or more individuals, teams, or departments.

> *As I participate in a Heart Talk,*
> *I am experiencing a deeper level of listening*
> *and a release of unexpressed emotions.*

*A*re you ready to have your first Heart Talk? Here's how to facilitate one.

Have everyone sit in a circle or at a table, where the guidelines are introduced or repeated. The group's leader holds a small heart-shaped object. Pass the object around the circle as many times as necessary to ensure everyone has had time and a chance to share. A Heart Talk will end naturally when the "heart" has made a complete circle without anyone having something more to say. These are the guidelines:

- Only the person holding the "heart" is allowed to talk
- Talk only about how you feel
- Don't criticize, judge, or tease anyone for what they share
- Keep confidential everything that is shared
- Pass the "heart" to the left after each turn
- You can say, "I pass" if you have nothing to share
- Don't leave the Heart Talk until it's complete

A Heart Talk will create amazing results in a group: the safe expression of feelings, the "letting go" of resentments and old issues, the opening of a space to resolve conflict, constructive ideas, mutual respect, understanding, and a more connected group.

> *I am feeling free and optimistic as
> I willingly let go of any resentments and
> old issues during a Heart Talk.*

Week 45

Tell the Truth Sooner Rather Than Later

AFFIRMATIONS
for
Meditation and Reflection

I am actively practicing the habit of speaking my mind and telling the truth sooner, no matter how difficult the topic or circumstances.

I am regularly bringing up important information and telling the truth, which makes me feel relieved, energized, and healthy.

I am telling the truth as soon as possible because it allows me to deal in reality and find the best resolution.

> *In a time of universal deceit, telling the*
> *truth is a revolutionary act.*
>
> —UNKNOWN
> (Often credited to George Orwell)

*I*t takes energy to withhold the truth, keep a secret, or keep up an act. We avoid telling the truth sometimes because the consequences are uncomfortable. We don't want to hurt someone's feelings or we're afraid they will get upset or even angry. But, when no one is telling the truth, we can't solve anything from a basis in reality. We just waste energy that could be better focused on creating more success in all areas of our lives. We can accomplish so much more when vital information is shared and acted upon.

For each of us, there are three areas that need to be shared most: resentments that have built up, unmet needs and demands underlying those resentments, and unexpressed gratitude.

Telling the truth when it's uncomfortable is one of the most valuable practices, yet it's one of the most difficult to do. We worry so much about hurting other people's feelings that we don't express our own true feelings and we hurt ourselves instead. But it doesn't have to be that way—we can change.

> *I am actively practicing the habit of speaking my*
> *mind and telling the truth sooner, no matter*
> *how difficult the topic or circumstances.*

There's no perfect time to tell the truth, but becoming accustomed to telling it sooner rather than later is one of the most important success skills you will learn. It can be uncomfortable. It will likely cause reactions—sometimes emotional ones. But if you get into the habit of speaking the truth as soon as you think it, that's being authentic. People will know they can count on you. Your intentions, goals, and plans will never be misunderstood. Others will trust you more because they will always know where you stand.

If there are so many positive benefits to bringing up the difficult and telling the truth, why then do people hesitate? The most common excuse is *I don't want to hurt anybody's feelings.* But what's actually happening is that you're avoiding how you will feel if they get upset. It's the coward's way out of having to put all your cards on the table. Hiding the truth will always backfire, and the longer you do it, the more of a disservice you do to others and to yourself.

You don't like it when someone is dishonest with you and withholds the truth. They won't like it either when they find out you hid the truth from them. Avoid all of that by speaking up as soon as you can. Done it in the right spirit—without being hurtful—you'll get respect for telling the truth.

> *I am regularly bringing up important information and telling the truth, which makes me feel relieved, energized, and healthy.*

ere's another thought on telling the truth faster. If you hold back because you have a fear of being judged, you will have to monitor your conversations, remember who was told what, and come up with excuses about why you can't do this or that. Simply stating your reason and moving on is freedom—it's powerful and shows very impressive self-confidence.

Finally, when you tell the truth sooner rather than later, you and those you live and work with can deal with the reality of the situation and find a workable solution rather than remaining stuck in some illusion that is being maintained by not addressing the truth.

> *I am telling the truth as soon as possible because it allows me to deal in reality and find the best resolution.*

Speak with Impeccability About Others

AFFIRMATIONS
for
Meditation and Reflection

I am in control of the words I use; I have mastered speaking truth and affirming life.

I am only speaking words that build self-esteem and self-confidence, that build positive relationships and realized dreams.

I choose to speak with impeccability; my words are truthful and have the power to uplift and affirm other people's worth.

Impeccability of the word can lead you to personal freedom, to huge success and abundance; it can take away all fear and transform it into joy and love.

—DON MIGUEL RUIZ
Author of *The Four Agreements*

*E*verything you say produces an effect in the world and everything you say *to someone else* produces an effect in that person. You are constantly creating either something positive or something negative with your words.

Successful people know that if they don't have control and power over their words, their words will have control and power over them. They know that to be more successful, their words need to build people up, not tear them down. They are conscious of the thoughts they think and the words they speak.

Words are also the basis of all relationships—how I speak *to you* and *about you* determines the quality of our relationship. When you speak words of love and acceptance, you will experience love back. When you express judgment and contempt, you will be judged back. Learn to speak with impeccability—find words that are true, that affirm other people's worth, or keep silent.

> *I am in control of the words I use; I have mastered speaking truth and affirming life.*

*H*ave you ever thought about the outcome when you say something about another person? In today's world of cyberbullying and online gossiping, it is all too easy to post rumors about someone else or unwittingly disclose personal information online or add pejorative labels. What people casually (or viciously) type often stays online *forever.*

This kind of language—often done anonymously—is not only hurtful to someone else, it brings you down in the moment and creates a general demeanor of spite and maliciousness that works its way into other areas of your life. This result is why spiritual teachers and writers throughout history have warned us against gossip, judging others, and speaking with malice. It hurts you, too, because it keeps you in a toxic frame of mind—preventing the good you want in your life from showing up.

When you speak badly of someone, it also leaves a lasting impression of you on others. People will always wonder when *they* will be the next target of your verbal poison.

To avoid these outcomes, focus the power of your words on appreciating other people's positive qualities rather than criticizing their faults.

> *I am only speaking words that build self-esteem and self-confidence, that build positive relationships and realized dreams.*

Ohne final but crucial point about speaking with impeccability: stop lying, even telling so-called harmless "white lies" and lies of omission.

Lying separates you from your higher self. Plus, you erode others' trust in you when you're found out. The fact is, lying is characteristic of low self-esteem. It's the result of your erroneous belief that you can't handle people knowing the truth about you. And that, unfortunately, is just another way of saying "I am not enough." Additionally, often times when we lie, we're afraid to face the result we'll get from telling the truth. We don't want to deal with the emotional reaction of our spouse, the censure of our boss, or the denial of our request from a retailer, agency, or official.

Why go through the psychological turmoil of lying? Why worry about being found out or suffer the setback to your self-esteem when you knowingly lie or live with the distrust you've created when someone recognizes that you're lying? Be at ease by speaking with honesty and integrity instead.

> *I choose to speak with impeccability;*
> *my words are truthful and have the power to*
> *uplift and affirm other people's worth.*

Week 47

Practice Constant Appreciation

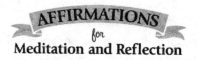

AFFIRMATIONS
for
Meditation and Reflection

As I express my appreciation for others, I'm enjoying being in one of the highest states of vibration.

I am learning to express my appreciation to others in their own love language, which is both fun and fulfilling.

I have taken a lifelong oath to own the magnificent being that I am, to appreciate myself, and to share that positive energy with others.

I have yet to find a man, however exalted his station, who did not do better work and put forth greater effort under a spirit of approval than under a spirit of criticism.

—CHARLES M. SCHWAB
First president of the U.S. Steel Corporation

People don't really complain about getting too much positive feedback, do they? In fact, they usually respond to appreciation with greater effort, more support, increased loyalty, and a better attitude.

Being in a state of appreciation puts you into one of the highest emotional, vibrational, and abundant states possible. Here are just a few ways to practice constant appreciation:

- **Play the "Gratitude Game":** Stop what you're doing and, for 20 minutes, appreciate as many things as possible— from the rain outside to the text message from a friend.
- **Spend time every morning in gratitude:** After repeating your affirmations, spend 5–10 minutes being grateful.
- **Make it a goal to appreciate someone:** Just like you set other goals, make it a point to appreciate someone for being a positive part of your life.
- **Adopt an appreciation habit:** Regularly show appreciation with a kind word, a return favor, or a nice email.

*As I express my appreciation for others,
I'm enjoying being in one of the
highest states of vibration.*

$\mathcal{G}$ ary Chapman, relationship counselor and author of *The Five Love Languages*, says that different people need different forms of communication in order to feel fully appreciated and loved. Here's how to get them right:

1) **Words of Affirmation:** If this is someone's love language, they feel most cared for when you share words of encouragement, appreciation, and love.

2) **Quality Time:** These folks feel loved when you share activities with them—fully present and engaged.

3) **Receiving Gifts:** People with this love language feel loved and appreciated when they receive gifts from you—anything from a small token to a major purchase.

4) **Acts of Service:** To communicate in this love language, do something for the other person such as running an errand without being asked or solving a problem.

5) **Physical Touch:** Just like it sounds, people with this love language respond to a pat on the back, a warm hug, a massage, or sexual intimacy. In the workplace, an appropriate hug, a fist bump, or a high five works great.

> *I am learning to express my appreciation to others in their own love language, which is both fun and fulfilling.*

To become a master at expressing appreciation in another person's "love language," learn what makes the most impact on them. Here's how to identify what works:

1) **Observe how the person interacts with others.** Because most people speak in their own love language, their behavior with others will give you clues about what *they* find important.

2) **Listen when they complain.** You'll find important clues in those things that bother them about other people or situations. If they complain when you work late, Quality Time or Acts of Service might be their love language.

3) **Pay attention to their requests.** People will often give hints that reveal their love language. If they ask for a hug, or mention how badly their car needs cleaning, or tell you that doing something together makes them happier than diamond earrings, they've basically told you which love language they speak.

4) **Take time to appreciate *yourself*, too.** Appreciate the positive qualities you have, the great accomplishments you've made, and the wonderful person that you are.

> *I have taken a lifelong oath to*
> *own the magnificent being that I am,*
> *to appreciate myself, and to share*
> *that positive energy with others.*

Week 48

Become Known as a Class Act

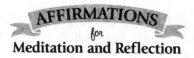

AFFIRMATIONS *for*
Meditation and Reflection

I am treating myself and others with dignity and respect, which creates a mutual feeling of love and appreciation.

I am acting with class by being courteous and grateful and always having a generous spirit.

I am treating others with high regard and making them feel nurtured and loved.

*In every society, there are "human benchmarks"
—certain individuals whose behavior becomes a model for
everyone else—shining examples that others admire and
emulate. We call these individuals "Class Acts."*

—DAN SULLIVAN
Cofounder and president of The Strategic Coach, Inc.

an Sullivan's strategic coaching program* teaches that we should do our best to act with class and be someone who attracts other people of class into our sphere of influence.

How can you stand out as a class act in a world where it's more normal to be average? Here's what Dan Sullivan says:

- **Develop high personal standards and then live by them.** Demand more from yourself—no exceptions.

- **Operate from a larger, more inclusive perspective.** Strive to be more understanding and compassionate of others.

- **Take 100% responsibility for your actions and your results.** Class acts take responsibility for their actions instead of hiding, blaming others, or making excuses.

- **Add something of value in all situations.** Pursue big goals that require you to grow. Bring value to the world.

> *I am treating myself and others with
> dignity and respect, which creates a mutual
> feeling of love and appreciation.*

---

* You can learn more about Dan Sullivan's coaching program at *www.thestrategiccoach.com.*

*L*et's look at other attributes that Dan Sullivan says are the hallmarks of class act behavior:

- **Focus on and improve the behavior of others.** Because a class act is a good role model, people around them begin thinking and acting at a level that surprises themselves and others.

- **Maintain dignity and grace under pressure.** You can do this three ways: (1) Remain imperturbable in the midst of chaos. (2) Maintain a calmness that gives courage. Your courage gives others hope that things will turn out all right. (3) Develop and express the quality of certainty that everything is going to be fine.

- **Counteract meanness, pettiness, and vulgarity.** The hallmarks of this characteristic are acting with courtesy, appreciation, respect, gratitude, and a generosity of spirit in all situations.

- **Expand the meaning of being human.** Class acts approach everyone, including themselves, as unique human beings with unique circumstances, and as a result, they constantly find new ways to make life better for themselves and others.

> *I am acting with class by being courteous and grateful and always having a generous spirit.*

Take a good look at your friends, partners, and colleagues —are they class acts? If they're not, that disparity is a reflection on you. Decide to reinvent yourself as a class act and see if you start attracting different kinds of people. Raise the quality of your attitude and elevate your behavior. When you become a class act, people will want to do business with you and become part of your sphere of influence. They see you as being successful, and they trust you to act with integrity.

Class acts teach others how to treat them—they lead by example. Of course, the first person you should treat with dignity, respect, and esteem is *yourself*—you'll teach everyone around you to treat you the same way. If you're lazy, always late, messy, and don't care about how you conduct yourself, other people are going to treat you the same way. If you were having the governor or the Dali Lama over to your home, wouldn't you hire someone to help clean your house and buy the best food you could afford? Well, why don't you do that for *yourself*?

When you start establishing high personal standards and begin treating yourself well, you'll get better treatment from those around you. Not only that, but you'll start being invited to places where people with the same elevated standards are.

> *I am treating others with high regard and making them feel nurtured and loved.*

Week 49

Develop a Positive
Money Consciousness

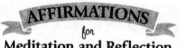

AFFIRMATIONS
for
Meditation and Reflection

*I am making positive choices about what to do
with my money and enjoying the energy of
abundance that it reflects.*

*I am creating all the money I want and need to
accomplish everything I want to do in life.*

*I am releasing negative thoughts and emotions
about money and feeling happy and free to
visualize my dreams.*

*A lack of money is not the problem; it is merely
a symptom of what's going on inside you.*

—T. HARV EKER
Bestselling author of *Secrets of the Millionaire Mind*

Financial success starts in the mind. While it may seem strange to have limiting beliefs and a negative predisposition about money, it's a fact that affects many people. Messages that we believe in childhood carry forward into our adult years. Then, our adult experiences often reinforce what we thought we knew: *Money is difficult to make and even harder to manage. Wealth is not for people like me. Life is hard.*

The key to having more money in your life is to change your money consciousness to a more positive mind-set, then focus on ways to bring more money into your life—and manage it wisely. Through the principles you're learning in this book—affirmations, deciding what you want, believing it's possible, and acting as if—it's easy to gradually shift your mind-set and develop a positive money consciousness.

What can you do to make more money? What does your daily meditation reveal that is a previously overlooked way to accumulate wealth? Can you recruit mentors or coaches to help you think like wealthy people do?

*I am making positive choices about what
to do with my money and enjoying the
energy of abundance that it reflects.*

What did you learn about money from your parents, teachers, and others when you were a child or young adult? Are any of these messages sabotaging your financial success?

Wealth brings pain and misery: It's not uncommon for a child to be exposed to volatile arguments about money (or the lack thereof). Those memories are painful and cause negative emotions attached to money.

Becoming rich would violate the family code: In many low- to middle-income families, there's a universal belief that rich people earn their wealth on the backs of the poor and take advantage of the average person. This isn't always true, of course, but in some households, being poor is a badge of honor and keeps you equivalent to your neighbors.

The "good life" comes at a sacrifice: Do you know how much your parents had to give up so that you could have a musical instrument, go to private school, or compete in your chosen sport? These messages of lack negatively associate wealth and ease with hardship and sacrifice.

Eliminate these misconceptions from your thoughts. Money is available in an almost infinite supply. What do you need to do to pursue greater wealth and earnings?

I am creating all the money I want and need to accomplish everything I want to do in life.

Bob Proctor, author of *The Power to Have It All* and a featured teacher in the movie *The Secret*, said, "The present state of your bank account is nothing more than the physical manifestation of your previous thinking." Let's turn around your limiting beliefs with this powerful three-step program:

1) **Write down your limiting belief about money:** *It takes money to make money.*

2) **Challenge it with statements that are actually true:** *For the right business idea, people will invest seed capital to get me started. There are many businesses that I can start on less than $500, such as consulting, network marketing, or becoming a service provider. I can get a promotion and a raise if I join the company's free management-training program.*

3) **Create a positive turnaround statement:** *Everything I need to make money easily is showing up at no cost to me.* Say it out loud with passion several times a day for at least 30 days and it will be yours forever.

Finally, use the power of visualization to see yourself enjoying the things that you want—as if you already have them. Add the sensation of touching it, feeling it, and hearing what it sounds like.

> *I am releasing negative thoughts and emotions about money and feeling happy and free to visualize my dreams.*

Week
50

You Get What You Focus On

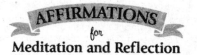

AFFIRMATIONS
for
Meditation and Reflection

I know in the depths of my heart that I want to have wealth and that it will become a reality.

I am focused on those things I need to do in order to acquire wealth and fund my future lifestyle.

I am paying myself first and putting aside a part of everything that I earn, which creates greater rewards and brings me closer to achieving my goals.

> *If no burning desire for wealth arises*
> *within you, no wealth will arise around you.*
> *Having definiteness of purpose for acquiring*
> *wealth is essential for its acquisition.*
>
> —DR. JOHN DEMARTINI
> Self-made multimillionaire and author of *Riches Within*

*I*f you want to enjoy greater cash flow and have a wealth of invested capital that pays dividends, decide right now from the deepest place in your heart to accumulate wealth in your life. Don't worry yet about how you will accomplish it. "You get what you focus on" is a rule that applies to almost everything in life, whether it's buying your first home, reaching your sales goal, building a business, or winning a competition. But it's especially true when it comes to acquiring wealth.

The first step to becoming wealthy is to make a conscious decision to become wealthy. The next step is to decide what "wealth" and a rich lifestyle mean to you. Hopefully, you defined your financial goals in *Week 3: Decide What You Want to Be, Do, and Have* and already have a vision in place. If you don't, do it now. You can't get very far in the area of wealth-building without knowing what you want, creating a goal, and visualizing your success.

I know in the depths of my heart that I want to have wealth and that it will become a reality.

*D*o you know what it costs to finance your dream life today—or in the future? To make decisions and plan for your ideal lifestyle, you're going to have to research today's costs and estimate your future costs. Most people say they want a life of luxury, but they've never truly defined what that means. Let's do that now:

- *Determine what it would cost to do or acquire everything you want.* You would likely need money for luxury housing, food, clothes, insurance, cars, philanthropy, vacations—in addition to continued investing or saving.

- *Visualize those activities and possessions in detail, writing down those details so you can research what it will cost to fund them.* For instance, while many people say they want to own a yacht, they have no idea what that really entails—including maintenance, slip rental, insurance, fuel, perhaps even a crew?

- *Determine how much you'll need to maintain your current or upgraded lifestyle when or if you retire.* Will your home be paid off? What will your monthly costs be?

- *Become mindful about your money.* Do you know your net worth? Do you have your estate planning completed?

To be financially successful, you have to know where you are, exactly where you want to go, and what's required to get there.

I am focused on those things I need to do in order to acquire wealth and fund my future lifestyle.

While paying off your creditors and becoming debt-free is a good first step toward better money management, this next financial rule will surprise you: PAY YOURSELF FIRST. Instead of paying bills or making new purchases, pay yourself *first* an amount that will allow you to invest for the long term.

If you don't have an investment account—mutual funds, annuities, stock-trading account—sit down with a financial planner who can help you establish one. Then, educate yourself about how it works, what happens to the money when you send regular checks, and how much you have to invest for it to provide a stable retirement.

It's quite possible that, if you start early enough in life, you could become a millionaire on your invested capital alone. The fact is that over 99% of millionaires are methodical savers and investors. Most of them worked hard, lived within their budgets, saved 10% to 20% of their income, and invested it into their businesses, the stock market, or real estate.

To simplify paying yourself first, arrange for automatic deductions of a certain percent from your paycheck for investments so you don't have to make a decision or remember to write a check every month.

> *I am paying myself first and putting aside a part of everything that I earn, which creates greater rewards and brings me closer to achieving my goals.*

Week 51

Make More Before You Spend More

I am focusing on my goal of being debt-free and spending wisely for what I want.

I have changed my focus from spending and consuming to enjoying what I already have.

I am always thinking of new ways to make more money by serving the needs of others.

Too many people spend money they haven't earned, to buy things they don't want, to impress people they don't like.

—WILL ROGERS
American humorist, actor, and writer

Successful people have mastered the spending game—they are wise about how they part with their money. Successful people pay less for things they want, they live below their means, and they spend as little as possible to accomplish a goal.

Regardless of where you stand financially—even if it looks hopeless—you can turn things around. You can still become debt-free and save more if you persevere and stay the course. Focus and you will start to see miraculous things happening in your life. When you change your focus from consumption and spending to enjoying and being grateful for the things you already have, your progress will increase.

You'll begin to measure success in debts paid rather than things purchased, and you'll be able to weigh all of your purchases against your goal to be financially secure and debt-free.

I am focusing on my goal of being debt-free and spending wisely for what I want.

*D*o you know how much money you spent last year? Here's a great exercise for self-discovery: Go through every room in the house—every drawer, cabinet, and closet—and take out everything you haven't used in the past year. Clothing, toys, car accessories, electronics, crafts, kitchen gadgets, doesn't matter. Put them all in your living room or garage, then add up the price for every single item. Pretty big wake-up call, right?

Overspending wreaks havoc on your financial goals. When you focus on consumption, you go into debt, you don't save enough, and your plans for accumulating wealth fall behind. One way to curb the overspending habit is to pay cash for everything.

Next, reduce the cost of your lifestyle. You'll be surprised at how much you can save when you take a conscious look at how you live. Make it a game to get top quality goods and services for next to nothing. Then get creative about saving money.

Here are a few more tips to get you moving in the right direction: Stop borrowing money. Don't get a home equity loan to pay off your credit cards. Pay off your smallest debts first. Slowly increase your debt payments. Pay off your home mortgage and credit cards early. *Now you have a plan!*

> *I have changed my focus from spending and consuming to enjoying what I already have.*

C ommon sense tells you there are only two ways to have more money: spend less or make more. Once you know how much you want to make, you can decide what product, service, or additional value you can deliver to earn that amount.

Here are some ideas:

1) **Do consulting outside your regular job:** If your employer does not prohibit it, you could begin recruiting clients in your area of expertise who need the unique industry knowledge you have. Write a brochure that details the specific things you can help with and reach out to your LinkedIn network to spread the word.

2) **Identify a new profit center for your employer:** If you know you could generate more money for your employer by leveraging untapped assets such as a customer list, supplier relationships, or obsolete inventory, you can approach your employer with a plan to get paid separately or even partner with the company—sharing in that new revenue stream.

3) **Do part-time tasks for cash:** Online portals like *Care.com, Taskrabbit.com,* and *Upwork.com* connect freelancers with clients who need personal organizers, project coordinators, and creative types to do single projects or ongoing work at their business or home.

> *I am always thinking of new ways to make more money by serving the needs of others.*

Week
52

Share More, Serve More

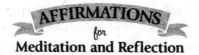

AFFIRMATIONS
for
Meditation and Reflection

Every contribution I make in time and money helps others and expands abundance in my life.

I am gladly tithing a portion of all I earn because I am grateful for the blessings I have been given.

I am joyfully serving others knowing that I always get back more than I give.

> *Give, and it will be given to you.*
> *A good measure, pressed down, shaken together*
> *and running over, will be poured into your lap.*
> *For with the measure you use, it will be measured to you.*
>
> —LUKE 6:38
> New International Version of the Bible

Throughout history, many of the world's richest and most successful people have also been the most generous givers. Industrialist Andrew Carnegie, for example, funded lending libraries around the world, eventually building more than 3,500 facilities around the world—launching what later became the modern-day library system. And ever since the first *Chicken Soup for the Soul* book was published, Mark Victor Hansen and I tithed a portion of the profits to humanitarian and environmental organizations. Because the series was so successful, we've been able to give away millions of dollars to hundreds of charities.

With all the benefits that givers say they receive from sharing with others, many people still find tithing—giving of your money or time to a religious organization or a charity—a difficult decision. However, tithing is one of the best guarantees of prosperity ever known because tithing regularly puts into motion God's universal force on your behalf and creates a spiritual bond between you and the God of abundance.

Every contribution I make in time and money helps others and expands abundance in my life.

*E*arning money and keeping score can be fun and exciting, but it's of utmost importance to keep in view the bigger picture: that the size of your income and your collection of stuff is not what creates the fulfillment you enjoy in your life. Wealth for the sake of wealth can lead to greed.

I love this quote by Junior Murchison, founder of the Dallas Cowboys football team, "Money is like manure. If you spread it around it does a lot of good. But if you pile it up in one place, it stinks like hell." When you share your success and wealth with others, greater success is gained. More people benefit. The positive outcome from sharing applies to just about everything, but it's especially true when it comes to tithing both money and time.

Bob Allen, the bestselling author of *The One Minute Millionaire,* didn't begin to tithe until he had lost all his wealth. Eventually, he reclaimed his prosperous life and determined that this time he would tithe. Today, he says he has so much opportunity, he couldn't tap it all in one lifetime. He also said this, "You don't tithe because you want to get something. You tithe because you've already gotten something . . . you tithe out of the gratitude you feel for the unbelievable blessing and lifestyle you have."

> *I am gladly tithing a portion of all I earn because I am grateful for the blessings that I have been given.*

"It is one of the beautiful compensations of this life that no man can sincerely try to help another without helping himself." So said American essayist and poet Ralph Waldo Emerson. It's true.

In fact, just like tithing, it's a universal principle that you cannot serve others without it coming back multiplied to yourself. People who find a way to serve as volunteers, missionaries, and mentors experience the greatest levels of contentment and satisfaction, as well as deep inner joy, in their lives.

When you volunteer, you get back so much more than you give—often in the form of better health and more personal satisfaction with life.

But there's another benefit to volunteering that's like a "special bonus" for people who are already successful or are on their way to success: volunteering enables you to meet all kinds of people you would never otherwise get to know. Building a network of important relationships is one of the keys to success—and frequently, the people you meet as you serve are the people who make things happen in your profession and in your community. These connections are unexpected career and business rewards.

The bottom line is, givers get. The world responds much more positively to givers than it does to takers. So ask yourself what can you give, share, and tithe?

> *I am joyfully serving others knowing that*
> *I always get back more than I give.*

WHAT DO **YOU** WANT IN YOUR LIFE?

Download our **FREE** Life Planning Workbook at *www.SuccessPrinciplesPlanner.com*

To help you decide what you want in stunning detail—in every area of your life—we have a free workbook and life-planning tool you can download now at *SuccessPrinciplesPlanner.com*.

It's completely free of charge.

This exciting and thought-provoking planning tool will even help you write affirmations that are uniquely your own—affirmations that will help you bring about the life you want!

After downloading and printing the planner, find a place with a comfortable, quiet environment (even playing relaxing music without words to drown out external sounds if it helps), and then clarify your vision of the ideal life that you identify.

The downloadable workbook will help you plan in detail the seven major areas of your ideal future life: work and career, finances, fun and recreation, health and fitness, personal goals, relationships, and your contribution to the larger community.

Download today . . . and start creating the life you want.

Visit *SuccessPrinciplesPlanner.com* to download it today.

ABOUT THE AUTHORS

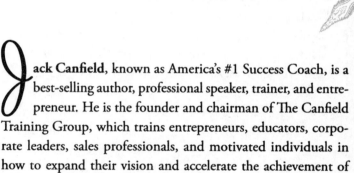

*J*ack Canfield, known as America's #1 Success Coach, is a best-selling author, professional speaker, trainer, and entrepreneur. He is the founder and chairman of The Canfield Training Group, which trains entrepreneurs, educators, corporate leaders, sales professionals, and motivated individuals in how to expand their vision and accelerate the achievement of their personal and professional goals.

As the creator of the beloved *Chicken Soup for the Soul®* series and the driving force behind the development and sales of more than 200 *Chicken Soup for the Soul* books, with 100 million copies sold in the United States (and 500 million worldwide in 43 languages), Jack is uniquely qualified to talk about success. Jack's nationally syndicated newspaper column is read in 150 papers. The *Chicken Soup for the Soul* television series aired on both the PAX and ABC networks.

Jack is a graduate of Harvard, holds a master's degree in psychological education from the University of Massachusetts, and has three honorary doctorates. Over the past 40 years, he has been a psychotherapist, an educational consultant, a corporate trainer, and a leading authority in the areas of self-esteem, breakthrough success, and peak performance.

The first edition of *The Success Principles* has sold half a million copies in 29 languages around the globe. Jack's other bestselling books—*The Success Principles for Teens, The Power of Focus, The Aladdin Factor, Dare to Win, You've Got to Read This Book!, The Key to Living the Law of Attraction, Coaching for Breakthrough Success,* and *Tapping into Ultimate Success*—have sold millions of copies and have launched complementary multimedia programs, coaching programs, and corporate training programs to enthusiastic individuals and corporations.

Jack holds a Guinness Book World Record for having seven books on the *New York Times* Bestseller List on the same day (May 24, 1998). He also achieved a Guinness World Record for the largest book signing (held for *Chicken Soup for the Kid's Soul*).

Jack is also the founder of The Foundation for Self-Esteem, which provides self-esteem resources and trainings to social workers, welfare recipients, and human resource professionals. Jack wrote and coproduced the GOALS Program, a video-based training program to help people in California transition from welfare to work, which has helped 810,000 people get off welfare.

Jack has appeared on more than 1,000 radio and television programs, including *Oprah, The Montel Williams Show, Larry King Live,* the *Today* show, *Fox & Friends,* the *CBS Evening News,* the *NBC Nightly News,* and *CNN's Talk Back Live,* and on *PBS* and the *BBC.* Jack is a featured teacher in 19 movies, including *The Secret, The Truth, The Opus, Choice Point, The Tapping Solution,* and *The Keeper of the Keys.*

Jack has conducted more than 2,500 trainings, workshops, and seminars—and has presented and conducted workshops for more than 500 corporations, professional associations, universities, school systems, and mental health organizations in all 50 states and 35 countries. His clients include Microsoft, Federal Express, Siemens, Campbell's Soup, Virgin Records, Sony Pictures, General Electric, Sprint, Merrill Lynch, Hartford Insurance, Johnson & Johnson, Coldwell Banker, Northrop, RE/MAX, Keller Williams, UCLA, YPO, the U.S. Department of the Navy, and the Children's Miracle Network.

Jack has been inducted into the National Speakers Association Speakers Hall of Fame, is a recipient of the Rotary Club's Paul Harris Fellowship, was awarded the Golden Plate Award from the National Achievement Summit, and received the Chancellor's Medal from the University of Massachusetts. He was twice named Motivator of the Year from *Business Digest* magazine, received the Speaker of the Year Award from the Society of Leadership and Success, and is a recipient of the National Leadership Award from the National Association for Self-Esteem.

To find out more about Jack's Breakthrough to Success Trainings, Train the Trainer Program, Coaching Programs, and audio and video programs, or to inquire about hiring him as a speaker or trainer, you can contact his office at:

The Canfield Training Group
P.O. Box 30880
Santa Barbara, CA 93130

Phone:
805-563-2935 and 800-237-8336
Fax: 805-563-2945

Email: info@JackCanfield.com

Websites:
www.JackCanfield.com
www.CanfieldTrainings.com
www.CanfieldCoaching.com

Kelly Johnson has worked in the publishing industry for many years; she was part of the sales and marketing team at HCI that helped the *Chicken Soup for the Soul* series become an international phenomenon. Kelly is the co-author of *Feeling Great: Creating a Life of Optimism, Enthusiasm, and Contentment* with Peter Vegso and Dadi Janki. She lives near the sea in Satellite Beach, Florida.

Ram Ganglani is an entrepreneur, businessman, and mentor. Dedicated and positive, hands-on and strategic, Ram's career spans sales, marketing, and communications, from Africa to Europe, from the Middle East to Near Asia.